# INSIDE THE
# COAL
# INDUSTRY

*by Tom Streissguth*

## Content Consultants

Raja V. Ramani, PhD, PE

Emeritus Professor of Mining Engineering
Department of Energy and Mineral Engineering
The Pennsylvania State University

Dr. John Grubb

Adjunct Professor, Department of
Mining Engineering
Colorado School of Mines

BIG
BUSINESS

Essential Library

An Imprint of Abdo Publishing | abdopublishing.com

**abdopublishing.com**

Published by Abdo Publishing, a division of ABDO, PO Box 398166, Minneapolis, Minnesota 55439. Copyright © 2017 by Abdo Consulting Group, Inc. International copyrights reserved in all countries. No part of this book may be reproduced in any form without written permission from the publisher. Essential Library™ is a trademark and logo of Abdo Publishing.

Printed in the United States of America, North Mankato, Minnesota
102016
012017

THIS BOOK CONTAINS
RECYCLED MATERIALS

Cover Photo: Tom Grundy/Shutterstock Images
Interior Photos: Shutterstock Images, 4, 44; Phillip Hens/iStockphoto, 7; iStockphoto, 12, 27, 40–41, 46, 86, 91, 94; Richard Bizley/Science Source, 14; Kentucky Geological Survey, University of Kentucky, 16, 56; Red Line Editorial, 20, 26, 70, 96–97; Everett Collection/SuperStock, 22; Everett Historical/Shutterstock Images, 29; Seth Perlman/AP Images, 30; Lewis Wickes Hine/Library of Congress, 32; Pictorial Press Ltd/Alamy, 34; AP Images, 37; John Guillemin/Bloomberg/Getty Images, 50–51; Jim Parkin/Alamy, 54–55; Jacek Sopotnicki/iStockphoto, 58; Eric Feferberg/AFP/Getty Images, 61; Jeff Gentner/AP Images, 63, 81; Crown Copyright/Health & Safety Laboratory/Science Source, 66; Mark A. Schneider/Science Source, 68; ADB/Alamy, 76; NHPA/NHPA/SuperStock, 78; Imaginechina/AP Images, 85; Elaine Thompson/AP Images, 89

Editor: Melissa York
Series Designer: Craig Hinton

**Publisher's Cataloging-in-Publication Data**

Names: Streissguth, Tom, author.
Title: Inside the coal industry / by Tom Streissguth.
Description: Minneapolis, MN : Abdo Publishing, 2017. | Series: Big business |
    Includes bibliographical references and index.
Identifiers: LCCN 2016945193 | ISBN 9781680783681 (lib. bdg.) |
    ISBN 9781680797213 (ebook)
Subjects: LCSH: Coal industry and trade--Juvenile literature. | Coal products--
    Juvenile literature.
Classification: DDC 338.2--dc23
LC record available at http://lccn.loc.gov/2016945193

# Contents

# 1 | COAL AND SOCIETY

A small car zips along the freeway. This vehicle is quiet—there are no gasoline-fired explosions powering the engine, no pistons churning or valves working. The car sends out a bit of a hum, like a big refrigerator. Instead of a smoky exhaust of polluting gases, the car emits water vapor. The driver checks his indicator—he's got a range of just ten miles (16 km). It's time to refuel. If this were an electric car, he'd have a long wait ahead—as much as three hours—at a recharging station. But there's no electricity powering this machine. Nor are there heavy batteries weighing it down. Instead, the energy comes from hydrogen. The driver pulls into a station and hooks up the feeder line. He refills the tank in three minutes. Then he's off again.

The Toyota Mirai arrived on the market in California on October 21, 2015. To celebrate, the car company invited the first 300 owners to a party in Los Angeles. The main event was a movie showing of *Back to the Future 2*, starring Michael J. Fox and Christopher Lloyd. In the movie, the costars use a tricked-out sports car as a time machine and set their destination 30 years ahead—to October 21, 2015. The message of the party was clear: the future is now.

*Vehicles powered by hydrogen, which is often produced using coal, are part of the future of transportation.*

Hydrogen-powered cars are the cutting edge of green technology, designed to avoid the pollution and climate change caused by using fossil fuels. The future of personal cars, trains, planes, and public transportation may be closely tied to hydrogen energy. And the single most important source for this clean fuel is a black rock with a long and complicated history: coal.

## COAL'S LONG HISTORY

Coal is a combustible black rock formed from fossilized plant matter. That is why coal and similarly formed fuels are called fossil fuels. It has a high carbon content and lies in long underground seams, or layers. Coal is abundant—there are huge reserves in Europe, North America, and East Asia.

Humans have been using coal as a source of heat for centuries. The Hopi people of western North America used coal 800 years ago. The ancient Romans used it, too, 2,000 years ago. Where coal lay near the surface, it could be easily mined and transported to nearby homes and forges.

During the Industrial Revolution of the 1700s and 1800s, coal fired new technology such as factory steam boilers and locomotives. It was also used to fuel heating stoves in the home. For a few decades, coal was the principal source of energy in the United States. At its height in the early 1900s, the coal industry included more than 12,000 mines that employed more than 700,000 people.[1] Today, the mining industry is the most important employer in parts of West Virginia, Kentucky, Illinois, and Wyoming. It supports thousands of families as well as local schools and

*Humans have long known that burning coal produces a high and steady heat.*

public works projects paid for by business taxes. Coal is still an important feedstock for electric power plants in the United States, China, India, and several other countries around the world.

## COAL CHALLENGES

Coal was once a prospering business, relying on a steady and strong demand for its product. But in the 2000s, mine operators found it increasingly difficult to stay in business. By June 2016, the value of coal from the Powder River basin of Wyoming had fallen to $8.80 per short ton

## How Much for That Coal?

The price for a ton of coal depends on its rank (quality or type), where it's mined, how it's mined, its heat content, and its sulfur content. High-sulfur coal creates more sulfur dioxide emissions and is generally worth less than low-sulfur coal. In general, coal mined underground is more expensive than coal dug at the surface, because the costs of underground mining are higher. Coking coal, used in steel production, must be low-sulfur coal that goes through extensive processing at the mine to reduce the sulfur and ash content. The most important factor, however, is rank. The US Energy Information Administration found the following average prices for the different types of coal in 2013:

- ▸ Sub-bituminous: $14.86 per short ton (0.9 metric tons)

- ▸ Lignite: $19.96 per short ton

- ▸ Bituminous: $60.61 per short ton

- ▸ Anthracite: $87.82 per short ton

- ▸ Coking coal: $157 per short ton[2]

Another important factor is how a buyer pays for the coal. Spot prices are quoted for delivery within a year. The spot price can change quickly, depending on the market price of coal, which changes from day to day. Most power plants, however, buy coal through long-term contracts. These may run for several years and allow the utility buying the coal a more stable, guaranteed price.

(0.9 metric tons)—a drop of more than 19 percent since the beginning of the year.[3] At these relatively low prices, many mines operate at a loss.

Coal is losing market share to other energy sources, such as natural gas. The main reason is cost: a power plant using natural gas is less expensive to operate. In 2015, coal claimed 35 percent of the market for power generation—a fall of 9 percent since 2009.[4] When the price of crude oil goes down, as happened in 2015, coal also loses its value. Tighter regulations by governments on coal use also make it less desirable as a fuel stock for power plants.

Besides the economic issues, coal also faces environmental challenges. As miners extract coal from the ground, coal mining radically transforms the surrounding area. Coal mines dug at the surface devastate old-growth forests in the Appalachian Mountains of West Virginia and Kentucky. The process of washing coal for shipment creates a toxic sludge that pollutes streams and lakes unless the operator safely disposes of the refuse. Coal burning itself releases sulfur dioxide and nitrogen dioxide into the air. These compounds react with rainwater to create acid rain, which can damage building stone and is toxic to trees and wetlands. A federal law known as the Clean Air Act of 1977 encouraged power companies to install special equipment to scrub these pollutants from combustion emissions. But as of 2011, more than half of all coal-burning plants still lacked this equipment.[5]

Coal combustion also produces carbon dioxide, which traps heat energy created by sunlight and, in higher concentrations, raises global surface temperatures. Global warming is an important reason many nations are trying to limit or phase out the use of coal as well as other fossil fuels such as oil and natural gas. Scientists and environmentalists have warned that continued reliance on fossil fuels threatens man-made climate problems such as sea level rise and water shortages.

Coal's environmental dangers, combined with the collapse in the coal market, are causing governments to refuse further permitting of new mines and coal-fired power plants. In early 2016, for example, the US government stopped issuing new leases for coal mining on publicly owned land. Banks see the industry as a bad investment, and some have stopped granting loans.

Nevertheless, coal remains an essential resource around the world. The coal business goes hand-in-hand with the rising demand for electricity. Power plants use coal to fire immense boilers

## Coal in BTUs

Although coal is categorized by rank, another important categorization has to do with British thermal units, or BTUs. The BTU is a measure of heating energy—one BTU generates enough heat to raise the temperature of one pound (0.45 kg) of water by one degree Fahrenheit (0.6°C).

The BTU scale allows the coal industry to compare the efficiency of different kinds of coal, and also to compare coal with other heat sources such as natural gas and petroleum. For example, high-grade coal can contain approximately 15,000 BTUs per pound. Lignite—the coal with the lowest carbon content—provides 4,000 to 8,300 BTUs per pound.[6]

Utilities also measure efficiency by the amount of fuel it takes to generate a single kilowatt-hour of electricity. For coal, the average amount is 1.04 pounds (0.47 kg), while for natural gas it is approximately 10 cubic feet (0.3 cu m), and for petroleum 0.07 gallons (0.26 L).[7]

and run electric turbines. When electricity use rises, so does the use of coal.

Increasing demand for electricity, especially in developing countries, means steady demand for the cheap and abundant coal that fuels power plants. Millions of people in developing nations such as China and India aspire to a more comfortable and convenient life. This means running electric lights, appliances, televisions, and devices such as cellphones and laptops.

Wind, solar, and biomass energy, although environmentally friendly, are not produced reliably enough, or cheaply enough, to compete with coal. In the future, as the market for these fuel sources grows, the renewable industry will scale up production. This, in turn, should lower costs for the end user, creating even tougher competition for coal. Syngas, which can be made by superheating coal, may also provide fuel for vehicles and home heating plants. Manufacturing syngas, however, is not an environmentally friendly process, as it relies on fossil fuel sources—as does the manufacture of hydrogen fuel.

## Things Get Hotter with Coke

Although most coal is mined for power plants, another important end use is in steelmaking. Approximately 70 percent of steel produced uses metallurgical or coking coal.[8]

Steel is highly refined iron ore. The ore dug from the ground must be converted using high temperatures produced by coal. In a process called coking, steel producers heat the coal using ovens that reach approximately 1,800 degrees Fahrenheit (1,000°C), in an oxygen-free atmosphere. The material is then sent to a blast furnace, where it produces carbon monoxide. The carbon monoxide reacts with iron ore to produce finished iron or steel.

The coal business is facing very serious challenges, including, in 2015 and 2016, a steep fall in the market price for coal. Regulations on emissions and on the mining process also put the brakes on the coal industry's growth. But the coal industry has improved its safety record, and coal mining is now safer than logging, fishing, farming, or construction work. As an industry conference concluded in 2015, "It is widely agreed coal is set to stay in the energy mix for a long time to come because there is no alternative solution that can provide reasonably priced electricity."[9] Coal mining will survive as long as alternative sources fail to meet the rising demand for energy.

# 2 | WHAT IS COAL?

Coal is a hard dark material that burns. It is mostly made of carbon, and it formed from plant matter, heat, and pressure over a very long period of time. During the Carboniferous Era, approximately 350 million years ago, mosses, ferns, and trees grew in abundance on Earth's surface. This was an era before plant feeders, such as dinosaurs, mammals, and birds, evolved and migrated over the planet's land surfaces. Earth was warm, water was abundant, and bogs and swamps covered vast regions. Dead plants gathered in layers in the wetlands, and when covered by seawater, the natural process of decay stopped. Thick layers of dead vegetation stretched for hundreds of miles. When covered by new layers of soil over millions of years, they changed form.

The first result of this gradual transformation was peat. This thick, brown mat of vegetation can be cut and removed from the ground like grass sod. Humans began using peat for light and heat thousands of years ago. Because compressed peat does not allow oxygen to circulate, it prevents natural decomposition. The bodies of people who died in peat bogs can remain intact over thousands of years.

*Large insects flourished during the Carboniferous Era, when today's coal began forming.*

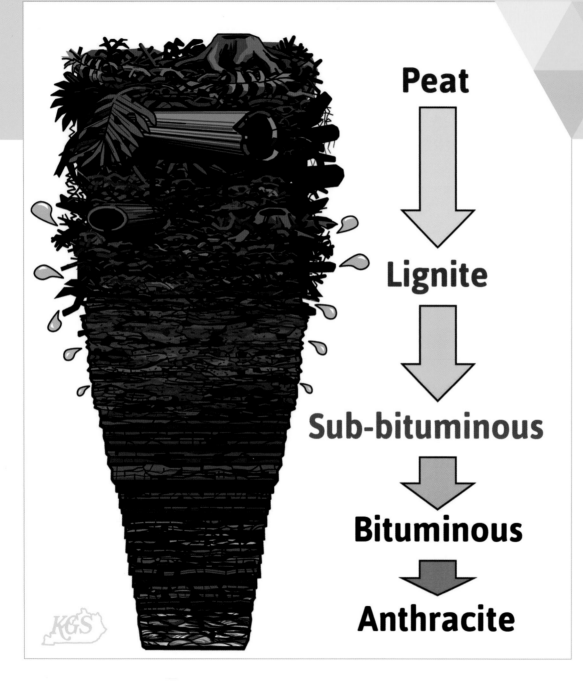

**Peat**

↓

**Lignite**

↓

**Sub-bituminous**

↓

**Bituminous**

↓

**Anthracite**

*With time, pressure, and heat, peat converts into lignite and then into higher and higher ranks of coal.*

When peat is subject to pressure from new overlying layers of plants and soil, it becomes lignite, or brown coal. This soft, crumbly rock can be easily set afire and gives off thick smoke when it burns. The carbon in lignite comes from decomposed, fossilized plant and animal matter.

Over millions of years, brown coal becomes higher-ranking bituminous coal, a relatively soft black rock and the most common product of coal mining in the 2000s. In the United States alone, mining companies dig, pulverize, wash, and transport approximately one billion short tons (0.9 billion metric tons) of bituminous coal every year.[1] The quality of coal for energy production depends on the level of the rock's impurities, such as ash and sulfur. Coal that has fewer impurities gives off more heat and less smoke.

More pressure, more heat, and more time create the highest-ranking coal: anthracite, a hard, shiny substance and an even more efficient source of heat. Anthracite is more than 90 percent carbon. Most of the US reserves lie in Pennsylvania. Bituminous coal—which is in higher demand as a fuel source—still underlies large swaths of the Midwest.

In the Powder River basin of eastern Wyoming, low-sulfur sub-bituminous coal exists in a massive underground layer covering thousands of square miles. These vast coal seams in Wyoming have two important advantages. First, they exist near the surface, allowing them to be mined by stripping away the overlying soil and rock. Surface mining is technically easier, and safer, than underground mining. Second, low sulfur coal also burns cleaner, giving off a lower concentration of toxic compounds such as sulfur dioxide.

# FINDING COAL

Geologists find the coal by doing surveys. They use drills to draw core samples from deep underground. The samples help them create geologic maps that show the extent and depth of the coal.

The mining industry measures individual coal deposits as resources and reserves. Coal resources are all areas of coal that exist underground. A coal reserve is an area of coal that can be mined at a reasonable cost. A probable coal reserve is one for which, with current mining technology, the rock can probably be mined economically—that is, drawing it out of the ground can be done at a profit. A proven reserve is one from which there is less doubt coal can be mined at a profit. A reserve becomes a resource again when competing energy sources are cheaper, and coal mining becomes unprofitable.

There's little new exploration for coal in the United States, where enormous reserves have already been surveyed. In many regions where underground mining was once common, companies have switched to cheaper methods of extracting coal near the surface that use new technology. In the state of Indiana, for example, 57 billion short tons (52 billion metric tons) of recoverable bituminous coal still reside underground. Only 12 percent of the state's coal reserves is reachable using surface mining, but approximately 70 percent of its coal mining occurs at the surface, using heavy machinery that was first developed after the end of World War II (1939–1945).[2]

## HOW MUCH IS LEFT?

Coal companies and the energy industry keep a close eye on the reserves to production (R/P) ratio. The R/P is measured in years. The higher the ratio, the longer it will take to completely extract a given reserve, whether underground or at the surface. When the R/P ratio declines, a company must find new reserves on its property, purchase or lease new property to mine, or slow production. Generally, the longer a seam of coal is worked, the deeper the miners will have to go, and the more expensive the operation becomes. The global R/P ratio allows for approximately 110 years of worldwide coal consumption at the current rate humans are using it. This is double the ratio for proven oil and natural gas reserves.[3]

Since 1980, the global production of coal has more than doubled.[4] Worldwide, production in 2015 reached 8.8 billion short tons (8 billion metric tons).[5] In the big energy picture, coal is abundant—but

### An Old Fire Underground

Underground coal mining can spark fires within the huge deposits that, in some places, stretch for hundreds of miles below the surface. In many cases, there's no way to put out these fires, and with plenty of fuel, a mine fire can last for decades. Appalachia's coal regions are dotted with small, smoky holes that provide an outlet for mine fires as well as toxic gases released by combustion. The city of Pittsburgh has been fighting coal fires for almost 200 years, which is a very brief fire compared with Australia's Burning Mountain—alight for 6,000 years. The fire may have been started by a lightning strike, a forest fire, or even a careless person who left a fire unattended.

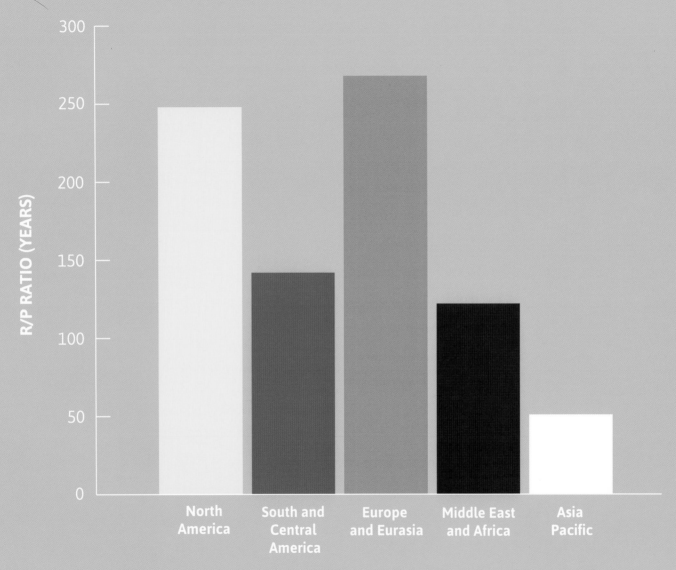

## Coal R/P Ratio by Region, 2015 [6]

R/P RATIO (YEARS)

300

250

200

150

100

50

0

North
America

South and
Central
America

Europe
and Eurasia

Middle East
and Africa

Asia
Pacific

**REGION**

the amount of coal is not infinite. If mining continues, at some point the world will reach peak coal. This is the year in which coal production reaches its maximum possible extent. After peak coal, production will decline. Countries that deplete their reserves will have to import their coal. This drives up its cost and increases the risk of a break in supply.

The dominant use of coal is for electricity production. Power companies rely on coal as a less costly fuel for their generating plants. But all fossil fuels are finite resources. If the demand for electric power continues, the energy industry will, eventually, have to develop alternatives.

## Peak Coal—Already Here?

The point where coal production reaches its maximum point and then starts to decline is known as peak coal. For any fossil fuel resource, a peak is reached when no new reserves are available. But some coal experts believe peak coal is here because of demand rather than supply. "The industry does not require new investment," said a 2015 report by the investment bank Goldman Sachs, "given the ability of existing assets to satisfy flat demand."[7] The key to the global market for coal is China, the world's biggest producer. But in China, the fast-expanding economy is also creating a demand for alternative energy sources. China put a freeze on new coal mines in 2015. According to one estimate, global demand for coal will fall by 5 percent between 2012 and 2030.[8] Falling demand around the world means falling income for coal producers and a bleak financial future for the industry.

# 3 | THE COAL REVOLUTION

Evidence for coal mining dates back more than 5,000 years in China. The Chinese once carved coal into ornaments and jewelry. Coal competed with charcoal, made from charred wood, to serve as a heating source. Mining coal was one solution to deforestation caused by cutting down trees to produce charcoal.

During the 1300s, English miners dug coal from rock outcroppings and underground seams that lay near the surface. In northeastern England, miners discovered shallow coal seams along the Tyne River. These medieval mines were built by digging a shallow, bell-shaped cavity in the earth. When the miners struck a seam of the black rock, they used shovels and picks to dig out the coal. They hand-cranked pumps to clear water that flooded the pits. The city of Newcastle became a center of the pit coal trade, exporting its product to the rest of the British Isles and the continent of Europe.

Pit coal was useful for heating iron forges and the big salt pans used to extract salt from seawater. Coal mining was a dangerous occupation, however. Ventilation deep underground was poor, and shafts were prone to flooding. Horizontal shafts dug too far into the

*Miners in Turkmenistan remove coal from a
shallow mine using centuries-old techniques.*

side of a pit could collapse, and candles used to light the mines reacted with a combustible gas known as firedamp, sparking deadly explosions.

## COAL AND STEAM POWER

Before the Industrial Revolution began in the 1700s, wood, charcoal, and coal competed as energy sources. In the early British colonies of North America, wood was plentiful and easily beat coal as a source of heat. As historian Robert Beverley, writing a description of Virginia in 1705, noted,

> *Their Fewel [fuel] is altogether Wood, which every Man burns at Pleasure, it being no other charge to him, than the cutting, and carrying it home. . . . They have very good Pit-Coal in several places of the County, but no Man has yet thought it worth his while to make use of them, having Wood in Plenty, and lying more convenient for him.[1]*

Commercial coal mining in North America began in 1748 in the Richmond basin of Virginia. With new technologies of the Industrial Revolution, coal emerged as the most efficient and economical source of power. Coal fired the steam boilers that powered factory machinery. Coal was an essential factor in the development of steam-driven locomotives and rail transportation.

Before the age of steam, textile and grain mills were built near rivers, using flowing water as an energy source. Running on steam, however, a factory could be located anywhere. Steam-driven power also allowed manufacturers to replace muscle power with machinery. There were 2,000 steam engines in Great Britain alone by 1800.[2] Steam also powered the pumps that removed flooding water—a very useful application in coal mines.

New uses for steam created a rising demand for coal as an energy source. Coal mining became an economic mainstay in regions of northern England, eastern and northern France, and the Appalachian region of the United States. Coal began replacing wood as the primary fuel for locomotive engines in the 1830s. In the United States, coal surpassed wood as a primary heating source in 1885. The demand for firewood dropped as homes switched to coal-burning furnaces.

## UNDERGROUND HORSEPOWER

In the 1800s, coal mine workers still used picks and shovels to dig coal. Manual lifts brought miners and horses underground. The horses hauled coal wagons along tunnels from the coal face where coal was being removed to the mine head, or entrance. Some working horses and mules spent their entire lives underground. If the mine had no horses, a pulley system hauled the coal to the surface.

## Coal and Power

During the 1800s, when steam-powered vessels replaced sailing ships, the US Navy needed coaling stations around the world for resupply. The first US coaling station was built at Key West, Florida, in 1857. In the late 1800s, the navy expanded its reach into the Pacific Ocean and throughout the Caribbean Sea. A coaling station began operating in the harbor of Pago Pago on the Pacific island of Samoa in 1878. In 1887, the United States signed a treaty with the independent Kingdom of Hawaii to build a coaling station and base at Pearl Harbor. In 1903, Guantánamo Bay in Cuba also became a coaling station. The need for fuel for military ships was one of the original motivations for the expansion of American power, which now ranges across the globe.

Mining coal underground has always been dangerous. Rockfalls, cave-ins, flooding, and explosions posed a constant threat to miners working under the surface. As the mining industry spread and new mines were built, the number of deaths and injuries due to mining accidents increased. As miners depleted coal seams, they had to work farther underground, increasing the risk of cave-ins and groundwater flooding. Firedamp remained a serious danger in a time when candles or kerosene lamps were the only source of light.

And coal still had competition, from kerosene and later natural gas used for home lamps. Gas streetlights became commonplace in eastern cities. But gaslights and their open flames posed a serious danger. In just one example, a fire started by a natural gas lamp backstage at the Brooklyn

## The Newcomen Engine

In the early 1700s, the miners of Cornwall in England had a problem. As they dug deep mineshafts to reach underground coal, the tunnels would fill with water. The only solution was to haul the water out in buckets or use hand-cranked pumps.

Local ironmonger Thomas Newcomen had a solution. In 1712, he built an engine that used steam to create an atmospheric vacuum. The vacuum powered a cylinder 21 inches (53 cm) wide and eight feet (2.4 m) long that drew water out at the rate of 10 gallons (38 L) per minute. The machine worked well, and in a few years more than 100 Newcomen engines were at work, making coal mining easier and safer. The engine also inspired the inventor James Watt, who patented the first steam-powered engine in 1769. Steam power for factory machinery then set off the coal-fired Industrial Revolution.

*Mining coal by hand was a dirty, difficult, and often dangerous process.*

Theater in 1876 killed approximately 300 people.[3] But the gaslight era lasted only a short time, due to the imagination and business sense of Thomas Edison.

## THROWING THE SWITCH

September 4, 1882, began as just another busy day in lower Manhattan in New York. But something extraordinary occurred that afternoon on Pearl Street. At three o'clock, Thomas Edison threw the switch on a giant dynamo. This machine could produce 100 kilowatts of electric power. It was powerful enough to keep 1,200 electric lamps burning in office buildings downtown.[4]

Since developing the first practical electric lightbulb in 1879, Edison had been experimenting with large-scale electric generation. At first, the city of New York refused to allow him to dig up the streets and sidewalks of downtown New York to install 100,000 feet (30,000 m) of conduit and wire. Eventually, the mayor gave in; by September, the wiring and lamps were in place, and electric meters were ready for service. Edison's first customers were business offices in downtown Manhattan, which replaced their gaslights with incandescent bulbs.

A few problems remained after the first day of commercial electricity. The power was not reliable, and there were frequent breaks in supply. Smoke was a continuous problem as well. The dynamo at Pearl Street ran on steam power, generated by boilers heated by coal fires. The plant required a huge amount of coal. The constantly burning coal created a pall over the neighborhood and grimed the walls and windows of nearby buildings. The station began turning a profit in 1884, suffered a bad fire in 1890, and was put out of service in 1895. By that time, much larger, more

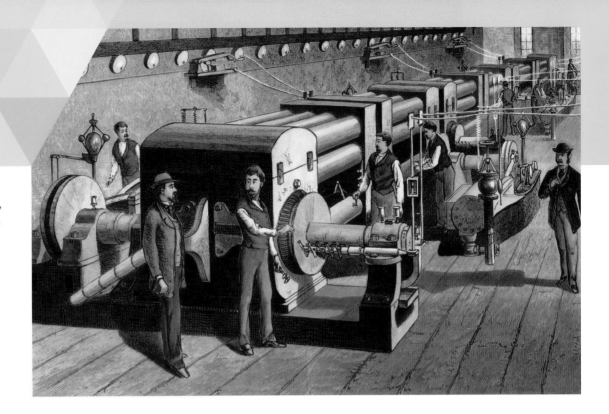

*Men work in the battery and control room at the Pearl Street station.*

efficient, and more powerful electric plants, located well away from city downtowns, made the Pearl Street station obsolete.

Nevertheless, the modern power industry was born at Thomas Edison's coal-fired Pearl Street station. A few years later, Edison gave his secretary, Samuel Insull, a difficult task: find a way to sell electric power to the masses. Insull built Harrison Street Station, then the largest power plant in the world, in Chicago, Illinois, and founded Middle West Utilities. His strategy was to buy up small local producers and merge them within a single business. By the 1920s, Insull was running utilities in 5,000 towns in 32 states, as well as a system of electrified railroads.[5] Through contracts granted by cities and states, Insull's company held a monopoly on local electricity markets. Government

*Workers take an elevator down into Peabody's Gateway Mine in Illinois.*

# PEABODY ENERGY

In the 1880s, Francis Peabody invested $100 to start Peabody, Daniels & Company, a business buying and selling coal in Chicago. In 1890, Peabody bought out his partner and established Peabody Coal. The firm began mining in Illinois and won a contract to supply coal to Chicago Edison, the electric utility headed by Samuel Insull. Peabody Coal prospered by meeting the demand for coal to fuel power plants. In the 1950s, Peabody bought Sinclair Coal and expanded into surface mining.

Peabody expanded to Australia in the 1960s and to Asia by the early 2000s. It is now the world's largest private coal company, operating in 25 countries on six continents. By one estimate, the company supplies 10 percent of all the coal used in US power plants. In 2015, Peabody sold $5.61 billion worth of coal and earned a profit of $434 million.[6]

But Peabody is not immune to a falling market price for coal or the problems faced by the coal industry. In April 2016, Peabody filed for bankruptcy protection.

agencies were allowed to control rates, while utility companies profited by avoiding competition. Insull's scheme also crowded out any home electricity industry that would have allowed people to generate their own power. Electricity was marketed as the means to a cleaner, more modern lifestyle. Households now had the luxury of on-demand illumination without the use of dangerous gas or dirty, smelly kerosene lamps.

During the 1920s, conveniences such as vacuum cleaners, radios, electric refrigerators, electric irons, and washers created a consumer-driven economy. Always-available electricity also powered the factories developed by Henry Ford and other manufacturers at the beginning of the 1900s, playing a key role in the rapid growth of mass-production industries. Electricity became an essential ingredient of economic development all over the world. Today, nations that can't provide reliable electricity to their industries and citizens are still at a severe disadvantage.

# 4 | THE COAL INDUSTRY GROWS

The demand for electricity brought a rising demand for coal. But just as life was becoming electrified and more convenient for the urban middle class, the coal mining business in Appalachia went through a wrenching period of labor trouble in the early 1900s.

The mines were located in remote, mountainous areas, where several generations of men and boys worked side by side in dangerous, unhealthy conditions. The work was tough, but the sense of community among miners and their families was strong. To represent their interests, the United Mine Workers (UMW) was formed in Columbus, Ohio, in 1890. Over the next decades, leaders such as John Mitchell and John L. Lewis built the UMW into one of the nation's most powerful unions.

Around the same time the UMW was established, Congress stepped in with the first mine safety law, passed in 1891. The law required ventilation in mineshafts and banned children under age 12 from working in coal mines. It did little to reduce the number of deaths, which exceeded 2,000 every year between 1900 and 1910.[1]

*At the turn of the 1900s and earlier, young boys were permitted to work mining jobs such as driving horse teams or sorting coal.*

The worst coal mining disaster in the United States took place in 1907 at the Monongah mine in West Virginia, where an explosion killed 361 miners. The Monongah explosion was not an isolated incident: the coal mining death toll for 1907 alone reached 3,242.[2] Three years later, the US government established the Bureau of Mines to study and solve the problem of mining accidents.

## THE COAL WARS

Organizing unions to demand better wages and conditions was not achieved without violence. To fight the unions, mining companies required their workers to sign what were called yellow dog contracts. Under these agreements, joining a union or even talking to a union representative were grounds for immediate firing and blacklisting. Many miners lived in company towns as tenants of their employers, who paid in notes the miners could use only at a company store. Without cash or savings, the miners found it impossible to travel even small distances to seek new jobs elsewhere. The companies hired armed guards to enforce the rules through threats and beatings. These enforcers occasionally murdered organizers who tried to recruit workers into unions.

The tension in West Virginia broke into all-out war in Logan and Mingo counties in 1921. Over five days, the Battle of Blair Mountain raged between workers and the deputies of the Stone Mountain Mining Company, as well as regular US Army units. The miners had rifles and pistols; their opponents used machine guns, artillery, and aircraft. The one-sided battle resulted, by an official count, in 16 deaths.[3] The number of dead may actually have exceeded 100.[4] After the miners surrendered, hundreds were put on trial for treason for taking up arms against units of

## Fighting over a Mountain

The Battle of Blair Mountain hasn't quite ended. People who wanted to preserve the site because of its historic value asked the federal government to put Blair Mountain on the National Register of Historic Places. The state of West Virginia agreed in 2009. Just a few weeks later, however, the famous battlefield came off the register. There is still a lot of underground coal in the area. Mining companies such as Massey and Arch Coal are interested in working Blair Mountain. The companies have done some surveys and excavation on surrounding land they own. But they won't be able to mine if the area becomes a protected historic site. As major employers in West Virginia, they persuaded the state's lawmakers to keep Blair Mountain available for future mining work.

the US military. As members became fearful of retaliation for belonging to a union, they quit, and the UMW nearly ceased to function.

*First Lady Eleanor Roosevelt visited a coal mine in 1935 and talked to workers about wages and working conditions.*

But the UMW survived and, by the Great Depression, managed to win good wages for its members. In 1910, a coal miner in Illinois made $2.56 a day or 45 cents for digging a ton of coal. In 1919, the scale went to $7.50 a day or $1.04 a ton—better than the high wages paid by Henry Ford at his Detroit, Michigan, car factories.[5] Wages stagnated through the Depression but continued rising after World War II (1939–1945). By 2014, the average wage for those employed in the coal mining industry had reached $82,058, as compared with the average for all other workers in the United States of $49,700.[6]

In the meantime, the federal government has adopted a series of mine safety laws. In 1941,

Congress authorized the first federal inspections of coal mines. After the end of World War II, coal mining companies began using heavy machinery for underground extraction. The miner's pick and shovel gradually went out of use. Coal miners became equipment operators trained to keep the machinery, as well as ventilation and electric water pumps, up and running.

## Miners and Health Care

In the mid-1900s, coal mining's dangers and health hazards prompted the UMW to seek medical benefits for members when they negotiated contracts. The UMW built eight hospitals and many smaller clinics in the Appalachia region. The group also hired doctors to work in remote and poor mining communities. Miners also gained from a 1969 law that granted benefits to miners suffering from black lung disease. In this way, the coal industry was a pioneer in employer-sponsored health benefits that became standard throughout the US economy.

New methods of bolting and reinforcing walls and roofs of mineshafts began reducing the number of accidents and deaths. In 1952, the Coal Mine Safety Act authorized the federal government to carry out annual inspections of any mine employing 15 or more workers. For the first time, the Bureau of Mines could shut down a mine or levy fines against coal companies for refusing to allow inspectors on their property.

Another law, the Federal Coal Mine Health and Safety Act of 1969, required two inspections at every surface mine, and four at every underground mine, every year. This law also set up a disability fund for miners suffering from coal worker's pneumoconiosis, or black lung disease, a dangerous lung condition caused by inhaling coal dust.

## COAL POWER IN THE 1900s AND TODAY

The demand for coal follows the demand for electricity, as coal has always been the cheapest source of power for electric plants. The use of coal for home heating tailed off in the 1930s, replaced by natural-gas-fired heaters. Locomotives switched from coal to diesel fuel by the 1940s. By 2016, coal was providing approximately 32 percent of the fuel used in US electricity plants.[7] For the first time, natural gas held a larger market share in the power industry than coal.

Nuclear-powered generating stations began operating in the 1950s. The power industry saw nuclear as a cheaper, cleaner alternative, but nuclear had its own problems. A serious accident

## The Last Mine

The first commercial coal industry arose in England. Coal fueled the British Empire's rise to global power. The coal industry sustained the British through two world wars in the 1900s. At its peak, British coal mining employed more than one million workers.[8] But in the 2000s, underground mining gradually came to an end. Imported coal from Russia, the United States, and Colombia—still needed for power generation—had become cheaper.

The Kellingley colliery, the last underground coal mine in the United Kingdom, shut down in December 2015. The closing was a serious blow to the Yorkshire community surrounding Kellingley, where miners held secure jobs paying good wages. Some collieries in the region had their own social clubs and bands and helped support schools and hospitals. But despite protests and strikes by the miners to prevent the closings, the economics of coal mining are changing in the United Kingdom. Before Kellingley, a long list of Yorkshire collieries shut down, including Hatfield in 2015, Maltby in 2013, and Rossington in 2007. Several abandoned coal mines, as well as old copper, tin, lead, and manganese pits, have become tourist attractions.

*Coal is easily stored in piles onsite before it is used in power plants and factories.*

occurred at the Three Mile Island reactor in Pennsylvania in 1979, and a fire destroyed another reactor at Chernobyl in the Soviet Union in 1986. The fire released a cloud of radiation that forced the Soviet government to evacuate more than 300,000 people living near the plant.[9] The long-term, safe disposal of nuclear waste still presents a difficult problem for utility companies that operate nuclear plants.

Natural gas arose as an alternative fuel for power stations in the 1970s. The competition between gas and coal as feedstock for power plants remains an important factor in the outlook for the coal mining industry. In addition to its lower cost, coal had some important advantages over natural gas. Coal can be stored onsite at power plants and used as needed, while gas must be sent by pipeline and can only be stored in tanks on a limited basis. For this reason, the fuel supply for a gas-fired plant is vulnerable to disruptions through pipeline breaks, leaks, and other system failures. For utility companies, a constantly reliable flow of electricity to customers is an absolute must. A downside to the coal business is the high cost of moving the raw material from the mine to the end user. In the United States, for example, the Union Pacific and the Burlington Northern Santa Fe are the two principal railroads moving coal from the Powder River Basin in Wyoming and Montana to the power plants of the east and southeast. Coal companies have no alternative choices for transportation and must pay whatever the railroads charge.

Powder River coal, however, holds important advantages over that of Appalachia. In the West, all mining is surface mining, which means easier access to the resource and lower labor costs per ton to extract it. In addition, the coal from the Powder River basin has a lower sulfur content than coal mined in most of Appalachia or Illinois. This allows power plants to spend less on the required scrubbers that rid the coal of sulfur, and it has brought lower sulfur dioxide emissions, less acid rain, and generally cleaner air around power plants using it.

Since western coal has a lower carbon content, however, power plants need to use more of it to generate the same amount of heat and electricity. This means increased carbon dioxide emissions and a heavier contribution to greenhouse gas levels. If the government begins limiting these emissions by law, utility companies will face another dilemma in sourcing their fuel.

## COAL AROUND THE WORLD

At the turn of the 2000s, energy demand in China and other developing countries was growing rapidly, along with their economies. In 2016 in India, coal provided approximately 61 percent of the fuel for the country's electricity plants, while hydropower provided 14 percent, renewable sources 14 percent, natural gas 8 percent, nuclear power 2 percent, and oil less than 1 percent in 2016.[10] In 2012, China accounted for 49 percent of global coal consumption, meaning a single nation uses almost as much coal as the rest of the world combined.[11] In other developing nations, such as India and Indonesia, coal also provides the cheapest and most abundant energy source. Power plants that use coal as fuel are also cheaper to build.

## Trouble in Heyuan

On April 12, 2015, a crowd of 10,000 people gathered in the streets of Heyuan, a city in the Guangdong Province of eastern China. This was not a political protest, nor a demand for better wages or working conditions. Instead, the people of Heyuan were demonstrating against the air they were breathing.

A coal-fired electric plant operating since 2008 had turned the skies over Heyuan dark and smoggy. In Heyuan and other Chinese cities, many people wear surgical masks when they leave their homes. They're not ill—they simply don't want to breathe in the particulates and smoke that foul their air.

When city leaders announced plans to expand the Heyuan plant, a petition began circulating. During the protest march, one woman commented: "This is not just a small fraction of people with an ulterior motive but a concrete outpouring of public opinion from the entire Heyuan public. From babies to the elderly, everyone is appealing to our government to stop polluting our sky."[12]

China, India, and many other countries place a high priority on economic development. Continued growth means more jobs, higher wages, and, in general, less political turmoil. Supply still does not always meet demand. In India, electric capacity has been stretched to the limit; rolling blackouts, used by electric utilities to lessen burdens on the power grid, are an everyday occurrence.

In India, coal is more abundant than oil or natural gas. India has built new coal mines to reduce dependence on imported energy. In a densely populated country, however, landowners resist selling or leasing their land to mining companies. In addition, air pollution increases when new mines are dug and new coal-fired plants are built.

Air quality has become a big problem in many Chinese cities, and the Chinese government has begun to address it. China suspended approvals for new coal mines in 2016. The Chinese government has taken initiatives encouraging the use of renewable energy such as solar and wind power. China also has become a global leader in a group of new energy technologies, together known as clean coal. But coal-fired plants and coal mining still present a range of environmental and safety issues. These problems threaten the future of the coal business and are prompting the inventors of today to search for alternatives.

# 5 | DIGGING COAL

Today, there are two basic methods of mining coal—surface mining and underground mining. Surface, or "strip," coal mining, which began near Danville, Illinois, in 1866, is technically easier. Although coal companies must make a big investment in machinery and vehicles, they can operate surface mines with fewer miners and save on the cost of labor.

Surface mining can take place when the coal is less than 200 feet (60 m) underground. Enormous dragline cranes and bulldozers remove the topsoil and layers of rock to expose coal seams. Large power shovels extract the coal from the seams and load enormous trucks. These vehicles bring the coal to a processing center, where it is separated from non-coal material and prepared for shipment.

Coal companies use contour or bench mining when a long seam of coal runs horizontally through an accessible hillside. Bulldozers and graders build an access road near the coal face, which is exposed by excavation or explosives. Mining equipment then travels along the bench, or horizontal seam, to excavate the coal. As the seam is worked, it becomes more difficult for excavators to safely bring out the coal. Miners can then

*A dragline crane works a surface coal mine.*

## Coal Goes High Tech

Computerized systems have become common in coal mining. Global Positioning System (GPS) satellites help operators map and plan their underground mines. Computers monitor the extraction of coal and track the production level as the coal moves out of the mine. The Groundhog robot, with a night vision camera and a gyroscope, can travel underground to monitor levels of oxygen, methane, and carbon monoxide. A smaller version, known as the Cave Crawler, can measure the size and stability of small, abandoned mineshafts. Someday, the work of coal mining may be completely automated, using wireless communication and excavating robots.

use enormous, corkscrew-shaped drills known as augers to continue production. Eventually, the soil and rock originally excavated can be used to backfill the depleted seam and restore the land's natural contour.

While surface mining, coal operators have an obligation to reduce the environmental impact as much as possible. A federal law known as the Surface Mining Control and Reclamation Act, passed in 1977, requires restoration of land disturbed by surface mining. State laws spell out the restrictions on noise, blast vibrations, dust, and disturbance of wildlife habitat. The costs of restoration are high, and these problems grow more complicated and expensive with mountaintop removal mining, which occurs in the Appalachian region.

## MOUNTAINTOP MINING

In mountaintop surface mining, coal companies use ammonium nitrate/fuel oil (ANFO) explosive. The ANFO is used to expose large areas of coal under mountain peaks and hilltops. The heavy blasting exposes coal seams, which can then be extracted by machinery. It also creates enormous amounts of rock and soil spill, which the excavators must truck off the mountain or deposit in adjoining valleys.

Mountaintop mining devastates forests as well as the animals that depend on wooded areas for food and shelter. Landfills grow high near the mountain. As trees and undergrowth are removed, the land begins to erode. With no vegetation or topsoil to hold rainwater, flooding from higher elevations washes out the local roads and can endanger homes situated downhill.

Mining companies have taken some steps to limit the damages from mountaintop operations. By federal law, mining companies must submit an environmental impact statement before starting a mountaintop removal project. On environmental grounds, the state can refuse to issue a permit for the project. In addition, according to the Clean Water Act, mining companies must file an explanation of how they will avoid dumping pollutants into nearby streams and rivers. Nevertheless, mountaintop mining has raised bitter

## Big Machines

The coal mining industry uses some of the world's biggest earth-moving equipment. Articulated dump trucks are built for rough terrain, with a hinge between the cab and the dump box. Dragline cranes, which strip rock and soil, weigh up to 14,300 short tons (13,000 metric tons). Scrapers move on huge tires, loading and unloading massive loads of earth around a mine site.

The Big Hog started on the job in 1962 at Peabody Coal's Sinclair Mine. This Bucyrus 3850-B Power Shovel had a bucket size of 115 cubic yards (88 cu m) and was the biggest shovel in the world. In the 1980s, the Big Hog was retired and buried with honors on mine property.

*Workers get into an elevator in a Polish mine.*

controversies and protests in communities directly affected.

## MINING UNDERGROUND

Taking coal from underneath the surface is more expensive, hazardous, and labor-intensive than surface mining. To access underground coal, miners must build shafts, both to get to the coal seams and to ventilate the rooms and tunnels where they have to work.

If they can reach a coal seam from the side of a hill or valley, miners can use a drift mine, which is dug horizontally, or a slope mine, which runs gradually downhill from the surface. Once they reach the seam, the miners dig a series of rooms and then set up machinery to remove the coal. For structural support, pillars of coal are left in place at regular intervals. The deeper the mine goes, the more support is needed, and the larger the pillars have to be.

51

## Working the Longwall

The motorized shearer is a large and expensive machine used underground to extract coal from horizontal seams. These devices have a large set of teeth set on a rotating drum. They allow longwall mining, in which coal is stripped from a wall and placed onto conveyors to the surface. Sensors in the machine detect the location and amount of the remaining coal. Shields protect the machinery from the mine roof, which is allowed to collapse behind the machine as the coal seam is depleted. The miners in longwall mining operate the machinery and never need to use a shovel or a pick. Longwall mining equipment is more expensive than room and pillar mining equipment, but the rate of recovery of coal is higher and the cost per ton mined is less than in most room and pillar mines.

Pumps are placed to remove water that floods from underground reservoirs or enters the mine from the surface.

Shaft mines are dug vertically. From the shaft, miners use machinery to dig out underground roads at the proper depth to reach the coal. An elevator is used to bring miners and equipment into and out of the mine. The miners extract coal from the rooms, leaving the necessary pillars in place for roof support and installing bolts to reinforce the ceilings. As the mining rooms reach farther out from the shaft, the miners install a conveyer or coal shuttles that run on rails to bring the mined coal out from the seam.

Deep shaft mines may reach as far as 1,200 feet (370 m) underground. The largest have hundreds of rooms and tunnels and a complex network of roads, along with lighting, pumps, ventilation equipment, and safe rooms the miners can use in case of flooding, collapse, or other life-threatening incidents. A busy dispatcher at the surface keeps track of the operations and controls the shuttles, conveyors, and elevators. Other supervisors track the amount of coal coming out of the mine, making daily reports to the company's management on production quantity and quality.

## PROCESSING

The black rock coming out of a coal mine—called run of mine (ROM) coal—is not yet ready for use. The ROM coal contains impurities such as ash and sulfur. These lower the BTU value and cause burning coal to release heavy amounts of smoke and toxic fumes.

There are several steps to coal processing. A feeder/breaker is a heavy drum with metal teeth that breaks down the larger rocks. A sizer then further crushes the rocks before a screener separates coarse and fine coal. Washing the coal separates any remaining dirt or rock particles. This lightens the weight of the coal and allows it to burn more efficiently in steam plants. At some processing plants, hydrogen, oxygen, and other gases are removed from the coal. This process increases the percentage of carbon in the rock so that it can serve as coke in blast furnaces to convert iron ore to steel. Once processing is done, the operator weighs the coal and prepares it for transport.

*Reclamation in progress at the Eagle Butte mine in Wyoming*

## LAND RECLAMATION

Companies plan for reclamation before and during mining. During surface mining, coal companies may try to prevent soil erosion by controlling flooding and the movement of rain-loosened soil. Topsoil removed from the surface is set aside for later use. Through reclamation, mining companies attempt to restore the damaged land to its natural state. After a mountaintop coal seam is exhausted, earth-moving machines contour the earth, restoring the original hills and slopes. A layer of topsoil is returned to graded areas, and the ground is reseeded with trees and vegetation native to the area. If successful, reclamation can provide land suitable for parks, farms, housing, wildlife preserves, wetlands, or golf courses. In this way, the land can continue to provide jobs and an economic return.

A variety of coal mining techniques are used depending on the position of the coal deposits. Underground mining methods include shaft mines, reached through a vertical shaft, slope mines, reached through a sloping tunnel, and drift mines, which enter the hillside horizontally. Other mining methods collect coal from the surface. Mountaintop mining uses dragline cranes to remove material from the tops of hills or mountains. In contour mining, machinery including bulldozers follows a coal seam along a ridge. After other surface techniques are exhausted, high wall or auger mine techniques follow the coal seams deeper into the mountain ridge using large drills called augers or other underground mining machines. Area mines remove coal from large flat areas.

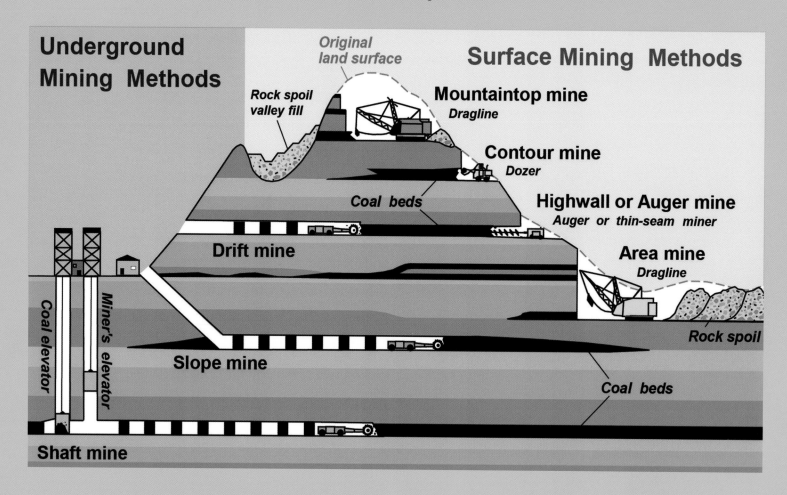

In the three decades after the federal government passed the Surface Mining Control and Reclamation Act of 1977, mining companies restored 2.8 million acres (1.1 million ha) of land.[1] This work has gone hand in hand with stricter regulation of power plant emissions to lessen coal mining's impact on the environment—although mining itself remains a hazardous occupation.

## The Black Mesa

The Hopi people have used coal for centuries. Today, the Hopi live on top of the 21 billion short tons (19 billion metric tons) of coal within the Black Mesa deposit in northern Arizona.[2] The coal lies entirely within American Indian reservations, and in 1966, surface mining of the Black Mesa began, under leases signed by the Hopi and Navajo tribal councils with the Peabody Coal Company.

Coal extraction at Black Mesa's two big strip mines, Black Mesa and Kayenta, has raised controversy. Many local people claim the mining is contaminating their water. During the surface mining process, runoff filled with debris, coal dust, and dirt reaches the groundwater. Tests conducted by the US Geological Survey have shown groundwater levels decreasing, and the percentage of sulfur in the water increasing. While the Black Mesa mine closed in 2005, mining continued in 2016 at the nearby Kayenta Mine.

# 6 | COAL HAZARDS

The day shift at the Upper Big Branch, a mine on the outskirts of Montcoal, West Virginia, began before dawn on April 5, 2010. By 7:00 a.m., more than 40 miners were at work underground, at depths of 1,000 feet (300 m) and more.[1] The shearers ripped black rock from the longwalls of sections HG22 and TG22. Coal and rock dust filled the air, and the noise was intense.

The fire bosses working alongside the miners checked their monitor readouts of oxygen, methane, and carbon monoxide. To be accurate, these devices must be recalibrated at least once a month. But it's an inconvenient procedure that takes time. The supervisors who direct the underground crews are under pressure from management to keep the shearers up and the mine producing.

David Farley, working on the water pump crew, turned to another man, Jason Stanley, and made a comment about the strange, still air. It seemed no air was actually moving through the mine, which meant a busted fan or another ventilation problem somewhere. Stanley just listened. His red hard

*A shearer has large teeth to tear through rock.*

hat marked him as a rookie miner who had been on the job for less than a year. Neither realized the danger they were in.

## A DANGEROUS BUSINESS

Underground coal mining has always been a dangerous business. Although conditions have greatly improved, modern miners still face the threat of cave-ins and collapsing walls and ceilings. They must also deal with a combustible material—the coal itself. While digging through underground seams of rock, miners can inhale toxic gases, such as carbon monoxide and hydrogen sulfide.

Methane, a natural by-product of coal mining, needs only a spark from a tool striking a rock or a short circuit in electric equipment to react explosively with coal dust. To control the

## Old Mine Problems

The long history of underground coal mining in Appalachia has left dangers for the people who live there. Thousands of old and unused mineshafts crisscross the hills and valleys. Many are unmarked and missing from surveys or maps. Each year, people fall into unused tunnels and vertical shafts. Floodwater containing toxic compounds often drains from old mines as well.

Incomplete or inaccurate mapping of the subterranean mine tunnels poses a hazard for those working in active mines. Survey work and mapping carried out by mining companies is intended to find abandoned mineshafts. However, only an outdated map was available and in use for a mine operated by PBS Coal at Quecreek, Pennsylvania. In 2002, Quecreek miners breached the wall of an abandoned, unmarked shaft 240 feet (73 m) underground. The result was a flash underground flood of 50 million gallons (190 million L) of freezing water. All nine trapped miners were rescued after a 77-hour operation.[2]

*A worker repairs a pump in a Ukrainian mine.*

amount of coal dust in the air, miners apply crushed stone and rock dust to the floors and walls of underground shafts—a practice required by rock dusting safety laws.

People working the pumps clear water from the tunnels. Water from underground sources, as well as rainwater, constantly seeps through coal mines. If the water pumps break down, as they did before the April 5, 2010, shift, the tunnels can flood, making mining impossible. The water crew must put on waders and struggle through icy water to repair the machinery.

In longwall mining, miners position the enormous shearer against a horizontal seam of coal. These temperamental devices are expensive, and they need constant upkeep and frequent repair. There's a big investment of money at stake. Taking the shearer or the conveyors down for any length of time means the mine is losing money.

At Upper Big Branch, the trapped, still air allowed methane to accumulate to dangerous levels. Several monitors showed the high gas levels, but the miners continued working. According to a later report, "The company's ventilation system did not adequately ventilate the mine. As a result, explosive gases were allowed to build up."[3]

Just after 3:00 p.m., a sound like thunder tore through the Upper Big Branch mine. On the surface, white smoke and debris erupted from the mine portals. Something dangerous had happened deep underground: coal dust ignited by a methane explosion created a more powerful explosion that rocketed through the tunnels with enormous force. Superintendent Gary May told dispatcher Adam Jenkins to order everyone out of the mine immediately. Jenkins began yelling over his radio. "And I hollered and hollered and hollered just, you know, praying and hoping that somebody would answer me," recalled Jenkins later, "and it never happened."[4]

## ACCIDENTS AND SAFETY

David Farley and Jason Stanley made it out of the Big Branch mine alive. But the explosion claimed 29 lives, making Upper Big Branch the worst US coal-mining disaster since an explosion killed 38 miners at the Finley Coal Company in Hyden, Kentucky, in 1970. Just four years before Big

A memorial outside the Upper Big Branch mine is dedicated to the miners who died.

Branch, another explosion killed 12 miners at Sago. That same year, a fire claimed two miners at Aracoma-Alma, both West Virginia mines. In 2009, however, the industry had a relatively good year for safety. In that year, the industry set a record-low death toll of only 34.[5] In the years since, the death toll has dropped further.

Congress passed the first federal mine safety law in 1891. In 1910, the Bureau of Mines was established to research mine construction and safety. Congress authorized federal inspectors to enter mines in 1941, and in 1952 passed the Federal Coal Mine Safety Act. This law allowed inspectors to shut down mines entirely for repeated safety violations. Congress was prompted to act by an explosion at a mine in Centralia, Illinois, that killed 111 miners in 1947.[6] The Centralia mine had ignored repeated warnings from inspectors about dangerous conditions.

The Big Branch mine already had a poor safety record before the explosion. The Mine Safety and Health Administration (MSHA) had found 369 different safety violations.[7] An independent report on the explosion found, "The company failed to meet federal and state safe principal standards for the application of rock dust. Therefore, coal dust provided the fuel that allowed the explosion to propagate through the mine."[8]

The Performance Coal Company operated the Big Branch mine. But Performance Coal was a subsidiary of a much bigger company, Massey Coal. The MSHA hit Massey with $10.8 million in fines.[9] Don Blankenship, the chief executive officer of Massey, was convicted of willfully violating federal safety standards. In April 2016, a federal court in Charleston, West Virginia, handed Blankenship the maximum sentence: one year in jail.

## WORKER HEALTH

Underground coal mining, even in a safe environment, brings on a variety of health issues as well. It can be backbreaking work, causing serious stress on joints, feet, and the spine. Breathing coal dust can bring on black lung disease.

## Relying on Contractors

Wages and benefits make up a large part of coal companies' expenses. Thus, employers often seek to hire nonunion miners, who work for 20 to 30 percent less than union members.[10] Union membership among coal miners has been falling for years, and in Kentucky the industry is completely nonunion: the last union miners were laid off in early 2015.

Coal companies also benefit by using independent contractors. A contractor works for a mine on an as-needed basis but has a separate employer. For some operations, such as blasting, a separate contracting company provides needed expertise, as well as more efficient and safer operations. But at some mines, contractors don't have the same experience as company miners. It can take years to learn the quirks of an individual coal mine. A contractor working at an unfamiliar mine may increase the chance of an accident that can cost lives as well as money. According to a report by the Centers for Disease Control, however, the safety record for contractors is improving: "The industrial-wide data indicates that contractor and operator injury rates have converged since 2005 and are now equivalent."[11]

*A technician in a British coal mine monitors the noise produced by machinery for worker safety.*

The federal government, as well as agencies in coal-mining states, have passed rules and laws to combat the dangers. Miners must don protective clothing, including hard hats and reflective vests, whenever they go underground. Breathing apparatus must be available. Wearable monitors show the level of toxic gases, including carbon monoxide. Miners also commonly wear brass tags that will identify their bodies in case of a fatal accident.

## PROGRESS SINCE BIG BRANCH

In 2012, Massey Energy permanently sealed the Upper Big Branch mine. The tragedy prompted several changes in the coal mining industry. Mines began using meters to gauge the level of coal dust underground. Heavy machinery now carries lights that warn when miners approach too closely. Laws prevent companies from retaliating against workers who warn regulators about safety hazards.

The MSHA also began enforcing the Pattern of Violations rule. Passed in 1977, the rule allowed the MSHA to shut down mines that showed repeated violations of safety regulations. In 2011, the agency used the rule for the first time, on mines in West Virginia and Kentucky.

## A Less Fatal Occupation

Coal mining in the early 1900s brought about deaths and injuries on a big scale. There were more than 1,000 deaths in the industry every year between 1900 and 1945. Since the 1950s, however, the fatality rate has stayed below 1 per 1,000 workers, and since 1985 the annual death toll has fallen to less than 100. The improving numbers are due to better safety practices, regulation, and inspections.[12]

Worker safety continues to be an issue in coal mining, in the United States and abroad. On an even bigger scale, business and governments also consider the environmental impact of fossil fuels, including coal. Although the power industry has made progress on toxic emissions such as sulfur and mercury, an even more important issue is the emission of carbon dioxide, which is a primary factor in the changing global climate.

# 7 | GLOBAL WARMING AND CLEAN COAL

The heat energy in coal comes from carbon. The carbon in coal comes from plant and animal matter that is preserved as coal forms. Carbon makes up as much as 97 percent of anthracite and 45 to 86 percent of bituminous coal.[1] The higher its carbon content, the more efficient coal is as a heating source. When coal is burned, it also gives off a variety of chemical compounds, including carbon dioxide. The carbon dioxide produces one of the most serious, long-term environmental effects of coal use.

## COAL AND THE GREENHOUSE EFFECT

Carbon dioxide is one of the most common compounds on earth. When concentrated in the atmosphere, it absorbs infrared radiation—solar energy that arrives in the form of light. The higher the concentration of carbon dioxide (and other gases, such as methane and water vapor) in the atmosphere, the more radiation is absorbed by the atmosphere rather

*Anthracite coal, left, and bituminous coal, right, both give off carbon dioxide when burned.*

# Global Temperature Departure from Average[2]

The 0 line marks the average global surface temperature for the 1900s. Red bars show years that were hotter than average and blue bars show cooler years.

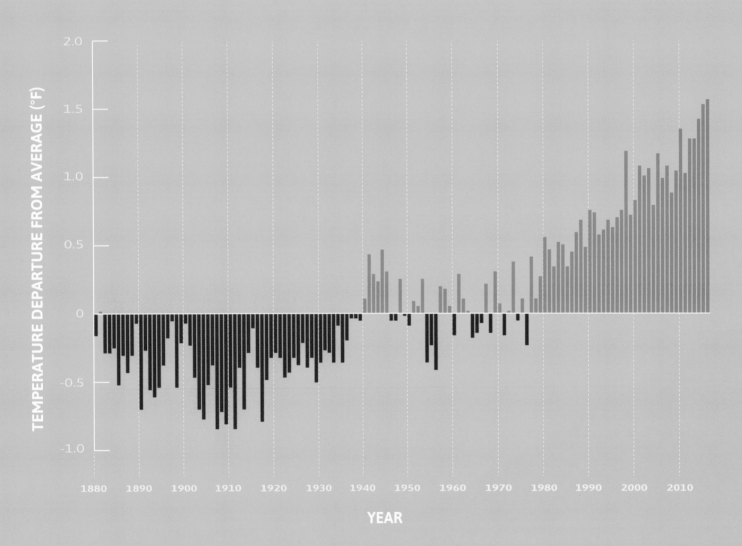

than returning to space. The net effect of more carbon dioxide is a rise in surface temperatures, a phenomenon scientists have called the greenhouse effect.

Earth goes through natural cycles of heating and cooling. These changes take place over millennia and even longer periods of time. They're caused by variations in earth's orbit and position relative to the sun, as well as changes in the sun's own energy output. But in a very short period of recent time, scientists have measured a rapid warming that is most likely not due to natural causes. February 2016, for example, showed the highest average global surface temperatures for any month on record. Surface temperatures were 2.18 degrees Fahrenheit (1.21°C) higher than average—not only another record, but also the greatest change from the average over 137 years of record keeping.[3]

Since the start of the industrial revolution, the burning of coal and other fossil fuels has increased the percentage of carbon dioxide in the atmosphere by nearly 30 percent.[4] Considering this data, and the well-understood greenhouse effect, most scientists find only a minuscule chance recent average global temperature rises are due to a natural process.

The correlation of rising carbon dioxide levels and rising temperatures has remained strong over the last 40 years, with some minor fluctuations due to naturally occurring temperature variation.[5] Nevertheless, climate change caused by human activities remains a subject of debate. A few experts believe that recent warming is due to a natural warming cycle, and that these cycles have a much greater effect on temperatures than do carbon dioxide emissions.

Coal is an important part of this picture. Coal has a higher carbon concentration than other fossil fuels such as oil and natural gas. In 2012, coal burned for electricity generation and other uses contributed 24.5 percent of carbon dioxide emissions in the United States. With other countries, such as India and China, relying even more heavily on coal for electric power, the global percentage has reached 44 percent. That means close to half the rise in atmospheric carbon dioxide around the world is due to a single energy resource.[6]

Carbon dioxide is constantly reabsorbed by the oceans. However, as the carbon levels increase, the amount remaining in the atmosphere also rises. A single molecule of carbon dioxide can endure for thousands of years.

## European Coal Conflicts

Europe is adopting renewable energy sources faster than most other regions. In addition, western European nations are not very friendly to the coal industry. In 2015, French president François Hollande announced that France would no longer invest in overseas coal-fired plants unless they deploy carbon capture technologies. But problems with green energy remain, and not everyone agrees coal has no future. As Brian Ricketts of the industry group Euracoal writes, "Abundant energy for all means using the cheapest sources as efficiently as possible. Moreover, the wheels of industry are oiled by competitive energy. Yet EU policy is to use more expensive energy: renewable sources such as wind and solar which require 100 percent backup. Europe has mistakenly picked these as winning technologies and is building a second energy system that doubles costs."[7] Ricketts and other observers believe the still-high costs of renewable energy are hurting European businesses that compete with rivals in other regions of the globe, including Asia and North America.

Coal mining, particularly underground mining, produces methane, another heat-trapping greenhouse gas. The rate of methane release increases with higher coal production, deeper coal mines, and more thorough processing and pulverizing of coal before shipment. In a single year, the world's largest coal producer, China, emitted 307 billion cubic feet (8.7 billion cu m) of methane through mining.[8]

## INDUSTRY SOLUTIONS

The coal industry is well aware of the alarming statistics, as well as the scientific consensus on the contribution of carbon dioxide and other greenhouse gases to global warming. Coal remains an abundant and cheap source of energy. But the pressure is on, in the United States and elsewhere, to switch to low-carbon and renewable fuels, or to replace coal with cleaner-burning natural gas. These trends may eventually reduce the demand for coal, as well as its value.

The coal industry has developed its own set of responses and solutions to the problem. High-efficiency, low-emission (HELE) power plants, fueled by coal, aim to increase the heat output of coal and cut carbon dioxide emissions from the combustion process. The HELE design for electric plants includes new systems for the burning of coal at higher temperatures and pressure. This design is already in use in Denmark, Germany, and Japan to lower fuel costs and increase plant efficiency.

The integrated gasification combined cycle (IGCC) relies on a process that converts coal or another fuel source to gas without burning. A gasifier combines the feedstock with air or oxygen

## The Turk Plant

The John W. Turk power plant in Hempstead County, Arkansas, reveals one possible future for the coal-fueled electricity industry. This 600-megawatt plant was the first in the country to use ultra-supercritical technology. In this method, steam is heated to more than 1,100 degrees Fahrenheit (590°C). The steam is circulated across the turbines at supercritical, or very high, pressures. The steam becomes a more efficient electricity generator, needing less water and fuel such as coal than at lower temperatures. The plant also has air quality control systems that reduce sulfur dioxide and nitrogen oxide emissions. Since the start of operations in December 2012, the Turk plant has become one of the country's most efficient and environmentally friendly generating stations.

under high temperature and pressure. The process breaks down this feedstock mixture into a highly concentrated syngas. This can be used to produce a variety of chemicals and fuels, including hydrogen, which burns without emitting carbon dioxide. Syngas can also be used to power turbines for electric power generation.

Underground coal gasification (UCG) is a way to carry out the syngas conversion before the coal comes out of the ground. Two wells are drilled at the surface—one for the injection of a mixture of water and air or oxygen, and the other to bring the gas to the surface. By controlling temperature and pressure, the operator manufactures syngas underground. It travels through the second well to a production site on the surface. There is no combustion, and any carbon dioxide emitted in the process can theoretically be captured in pipes and pumped underground into underground reservoirs. UCG also eliminates the high cost of transporting coal via rail over long distances. Syngas can be shipped by cheaper pipelines to the end user.

## PROBLEMS THAT REMAIN

Syngas and gasification may work on a larger scale as an alternative to traditional coal-fired power generation. But the energy business, and any other business, relies on a simple financial calculation: costs versus revenues. This is true for coal as well as renewable energy sources such as solar and wind power. If the costs of the process are not met and exceeded by the revenues it provides, the technology will not expand into commercial use.

China, for example, is placing a large bet on coal gasification, and it is planning on producing 1.8 trillion cubic feet (50 billion cu m) of syngas by 2020.[9] The most populous nation on Earth has limited reserves of natural gas. That means the Chinese must import most of this fuel and pay a higher price compared to the United States, where natural gas is abundant. China does have enormous coal reserves, but most lie far from end

## Coal Bed Methane

At one time, methane found in coal seams was nothing more than a safety hazard. A by-product of mining, methane was carefully measured and piped out of mines where possible. Methane explosions have always been a leading cause of death and injury underground. The physical structure of coal, and the high pressure of surrounding water, allows the rock to hold a large amount of methane gas. By pumping water out of coal deposits, methane drillers can detach the gas from the physical coal and bring the gas to the surface. Refineries can then process the captured methane into usable natural gas. This new technology is boosting the production of natural gas, which burns cleaner than coal.

users and thus cost a lot to transport. For these reasons, the Chinese see gasification and syngas pipelines as a viable alternative to natural gas as well as crude oil.

There's one catch. As the world's biggest emitter of carbon dioxide, China is under pressure to reduce its greenhouse gas production. But the aboveground gasification process used in Chinese plants actually produces more carbon dioxide than traditional coal mining. It also uses large amounts of water, which is in very short supply in the western half of China, where most of the new gasification plants are planned. Although gasification in China would help the country lower dependence on imported fuels, it brings a new set of problems to China and to the rest of the world.

# 8 | NEW COAL TECHNOLOGIES

The coal industry has come a long way since the first pit coal was mined 800 years ago in northern England. New technologies in the 1900s and today have made the job of mining coal and burning it at power plants cleaner, safer, and more efficient.

## SOLVING THE PROBLEM OF ACID RAIN

Scientists have long understood the environmental damage caused by coal. This includes the production of sulfur dioxide and nitrogen oxide by coal burning. When released into the atmosphere, these compounds form ammonium nitrate, nitric acid, and sulfuric acid, which in turn lower the pH level of rainfall, or make it more acidic.

Robert Angus Smith, an English scientist, coined the term *acid rain* in 1852. Smith observed damage caused to plants by acidic rain. A century later, scientists grew alarmed over the rising levels of sulfur dioxide and the acidification of lakes and rivers, particularly in New England and Canada. Acid rain was degrading forests, as well as stone buildings and historic monuments.

*Acid rain devastated a forest in Siberia, Russia.*

approximately 1.5 percent of the plant's exhaust and sent it through an ammonium carbonate solution, which absorbs carbon dioxide.[4] The plant compressed the carbon dioxide and injected it into a sandstone formation more than a mile beneath the surface. This process permanently prevents the release of carbon dioxide into the atmosphere.

Over two years, AEP captured more than 55,000 short tons (50,000 metric tons) of carbon dioxide. The company planned to scale up its system to capture 25 percent of its emissions: 1.6 million short tons (1.5 million metric tons) every year. The US Department of Energy, the federal agency overseeing regulation of the electric utility industry, matched AEP's investment, which amounted to $334 million.[5]

The experiment failed, however. The rates utility companies charge are subject to oversight and limits imposed by public agencies. Since no federal or state law was passed to allow AEP to charge its customers for the carbon capture and storage (CCS) process, AEP was unable to recoup its investment. AEP would have to operate carbon capture at a total financial loss or else shut it down. The Mountaineer project was the first CCS project at any coal-fired electric plant in the world, but it closed in 2011 after just two years of limited operation.

There are several other clean coal technologies on the drawing board. Whether these new methods are viable for utility companies, however, depends on the cost, the return from rates charged to customers, and the age of the plant. Gasification allows easier carbon separation, but it works only in newer power plants that are designed with the right machinery. In addition, they must use refined coal as a feedstock.

## LIQUEFACTION ACTIONS

Another clean coal technology began in the 1920s in Germany, where scientists Franz Fischer and Hans Tropsch discovered a way to transform hard coal into a liquid. The fuels derived in this process powered German tanks and planes during World War II.

Coal liquefaction begins with gasification. The syngas produced through gasification then travels to a reactor where it condenses into a liquid. The condensed liquid can be converted to fuels to power cars, trucks, and jet airplanes. In addition, steam given off by the process can power turbines and generate electricity.

The coal-to-liquid (CTL) process creates a more condensed exhaust stream. This allows emissions such as carbon dioxide to be more easily removed.

............................

### Oil Out, Carbon Dioxide In

Carbon capture and storage technology depends on finding suitable geology underground. Vast regions of sedimentary rock have tiny pockets of air that can be replaced with pure carbon dioxide. Carbon dioxide can also be pumped into underground reservoirs of saline water. Another possibility is filling depleted oil and natural gas formations. The energy industry has several decades of experience in pumping carbon dioxide underground for the purpose of extracting oil and gas. According to the United Nations Intergovernmental Panel on Climate Change, Earth has at least 2.2 trillion short tons (2 trillion metric tons) of carbon dioxide storage capacity.[6]

One of the major problems with CTL technology, however, is that it uses a lot of coal: one-half short ton (0.4 metric tons) of coal is needed for each barrel of fuel produced.[7] Building a CTL plant is also expensive, and the return on investment to the builder is uncertain.

A major upside to this technology is the promise of a synthetic fuel industry that allows the United States to become less reliant on imported oil. Coal reserves in Appalachia, Wyoming, and other regions remain abundant. Shipping coal around the country to plants that make electricity or syngas is more secure than importing fuel from distant continents, where transport can be disrupted by natural disasters or governments that impose embargoes and limit supply.

But clean coal requires enormous investment. Before implementing a new technology, energy companies must set large budgets for research and development. They then face the high costs of construction and testing before earning income from a new plant. With many coal companies in dire financial straits, and competition high with well-financed national programs such as China's, the outlook for new coal technologies in the United States is uncertain.

## CTL: Not Cheap

CTL is an expensive technology. By one estimate, it would take approximately $3 billion to build a CTL plant that could make 50,000 barrels a day of finished liquid fuel. When the price of oil is low, CTL doesn't make economic sense. The market oil price must rise to at least $70 per barrel and remain there for a long time for CTL to earn back its cost.[8] As of April 2016, however, the price of oil had fallen to approximately $40 per barrel.[9] With oil prices changing from one day to the next, the market for fuel remains uncertain. This discourages new investment in CTL and other clean coal ideas.

*A machine digs coal at a Shenhua mine in northwest China.*

# SHENHUA ENERGY

For 50 years, starting in 1949, the People's Republic of China ran on strict Communist principles. The central government owned all industries, and private enterprise was illegal. China began permitting small private companies, including mining concerns, in the 1990s. But public ownership has survived in the form of state-owned enterprises (SOEs).

One of these is the China Shenhua Energy Company, the nation's largest coal mining business. The company began in 2005 as an offshoot of the Shenhua Group. This huge state enterprise holds railways, shipping divisions, and power plants and employs more than 200,000 people.[10] As China's economic growth continued in the early 2000s, Shenhua prospered by providing coal to hundreds of new and existing power plants.

In 2014, Shenhua Energy produced 306 million short tons (278 million metric tons) of coal.[11] The company has also set up the world's first direct coal liquefaction plant, as well as a demonstration plant that converts coal to olefin, a fiber used in wallpaper and carpeting.

# 9 | THE FUTURE OF COAL

In the evening, an average neighborhood in the United States is humming with useful and costly electricity. Each home is running lights, appliances, televisions, and heaters or air conditioners, as well as devices such as cellphone chargers and laptops. In 2010, the average annual household consumption throughout the country was 11,700 kilowatt-hours per year, more than three times the worldwide average of 3,500 kilowatt-hours.[1]

Most of the power comes from commercial generators far from the neighborhood—power plants that are owned and operated by utility companies. In 2004, 625 US electric plants ran on coal; 1,143 ran on petroleum; 1,670 used natural gas; and 66 ran on nuclear power. There were also 1,425 hydroelectric plants operating and 749 using other renewable fuels. The numbers had changed significantly by 2014. In that year, 491 power plants were using coal and 1,749 were using natural gas. The number of renewable-fueled plants had risen to 2,674.[2]

## STILL IN THE GROUND

Coal will compete with natural gas as a fuel source for a long time to come. Part of the equation is a simple financial calculation

*Electricity from coal-fired plants lights the night around the United States and the world.*

## The Brighter Side

By turning on a switch or firing up laptops, each person in the United States uses approximately 3.7 short tons (3.4 metric tons) of coal for electricity generation every year. Many environmentalists favor phasing out coal production and enacting a ban on future coal-fired power plants. But when it comes to coal and the environment, not all the news is bad. Since 1970, the power industry has been successful in reducing the compounds that cause acid rain. Coal companies have restored 2.3 million acres (0.9 million ha) of land damaged by surface mining, and they have spent $7 billion to reclaim dangerous abandoned mines.[4]

around market prices. When the cost of natural gas falls, power plants that have a choice between gas and coal will switch to gas, which allows the plant to meet clean air standards more easily. When gas prices rise, they'll use coal, and the demand for coal will increase.

A sharp fall in natural gas and oil prices in 2015 and 2016, for example, also depressed the price of coal. In April 2016, the price of Powder River basin bituminous coal fell to $9.35 per short ton (0.9 metric tons). Coal from northern Appalachia, at the same time, ran $46.60 per short ton—much higher, and the most expensive coal in the United States—yet still half the price this type of coal fetched in 2009.[3]

This put the coal industry in a serious dilemma. If the trend continues, and the price for coal continues declining, profit margins for coal companies will vanish. The traditional business model for the companies—dig the coal out of the ground, sell the coal to utilities, and pay railroads to transport the coal to power plants—will fail to turn a profit. These companies will have to close or seek protection against creditors by filing for bankruptcy.

A train hauls coal from an Arch mine in the Powder River basin through Seattle, Washington, 2012.

# ARCH COAL

The second-largest coal producer in the United States, Arch Coal, began operations in 1997. At first limited to Appalachian mining, Arch soon expanded to Wyoming, Utah, and Colorado. The company became a leading producer of western low-sulfur coal, used in power plants to reduce sulfur dioxide emissions.

In 2016, Arch filed for bankruptcy protection. The falling price of coal had made it difficult for the company to meet its heavy load of debt. And Arch wasn't alone. Approximately a quarter of the entire US coal mining industry, by that time, was operating under bankruptcy protection.[5] Arch won't disappear; the bankruptcy law allows a company to continue operating while a federal court works out its debt repayments.

In January 2016, it happened to Arch Coal, one of the nation's largest coal producers. By filing for bankruptcy protection and reorganization, Arch can stay in business while a federal court decides how much of the company's debt—$4.5 billion—must be repaid, and to whom. Arch Coal was not alone; in the previous year its competitors Walter Energy, Alpha Natural Resources, and Patriot Coal all took the same step.[5]

This was bad news for workers who depend on the coal industry to make a living. In some parts of Appalachia, there are few alternative job providers. Agriculture is limited, and the region has little in the way of manufacturing. Coal miners who lose their jobs are hard-pressed to find others that pay as well, or for which they're as well prepared through education and training.

## Industry Finances

The coal companies' financial troubles stem from how the coal industry operates. Companies borrow money to pay the expenses of mining and processing; then, they repay the loans from the sale of their coal. When the price of coal drops, they struggle to pay the loans, until the day comes when they can't meet a scheduled payment.

Many coal mines, owned by Arch and other companies, still operate at a profit. If mines close, and the supply of coal drops, the price will rise. And power plants will still need coal, as more than one-third of the electricity generated in the United States relies on coal as a fuel source.[6]

## POWER AND THE PEOPLE

Another small but serious threat comes from people like Nick Dewey. He's a good mechanic who likes working around the home. Dewey is generating electric power for his home through a single homemade solar panel set up on the side of his house. A little blue box called a grid-tie inverter

Solar panels are being installed on more and more buildings.

allows him to return the power to the local electric grid. The aluminum wheel on his meter spins backward, and his electric bill falls. On sunny days when he's using a minimum of electricity, his cost goes to zero. "Don't just sit there, okay?" Nick advises on a YouTube video. "Make yourself some panels!"[7]

Solar power still has its disadvantages compared with power generated by fossil fuels. Those without Dewey's do-it-yourself skill must buy commercial solar systems and have them professionally installed. And of course, the sun has to shine, though new technology on the way

## Solar Catches Up

Although coal remains a big industry in some regions of the United States, solar power is growing in importance. The share of electricity produced by solar power is less than coal, by a long way, but the difference is shrinking.

One measure of any industry is the number of people it employs. The decline of many coal companies has forced layoffs. According to the US Mine Safety and Health Administration, coal employed approximately 120,000 workers in 2015; approximately 70,000 work in related industries, such as coal-moving railroads. Solar-related businesses, meanwhile, have caught up. The Solar Foundation estimates 174,000 people work in this newer sector.[9]

may help fix that issue. While Dewey was plugging in his first inverter, the solar power industry was still having financial troubles of its own, failing to reach a mass residential or commercial market.

But individual use also works for coal. Kyle Buck of Pennsylvania has a bin by the side of his house that holds two short tons (1.8 metric tons) of black rocks. From time to time, he shovels out a few pounds and feeds it to a coal-burning stove. A single ton of coal generates as much heat as 146 gallons (553 L) of fuel oil, or 20,000 cubic feet (570 cu m) of natural gas.[8] For home heating, coal is the cheapest fossil fuel. And in parts of Appalachia, anyone with a pick and shovel can simply dig surface coal out of the ground. It's not likely that a large proportion of city dwellers will go in for coal burners in their homes, considering the dust and smoke created by home heating equipment. But in rural areas, and in regions where gas and heating oil prices run high during the winter, cheap coal is a viable alternative for many.

Dewey and Buck foreshadow one possible energy future that may turn the current model on its head. Instead of centralized power systems that hold a monopoly on electricity and sell it at rates set by local regulators, millions of households may have their own microgeneration plants at home.

## COAL'S FUTURE: HYDROGEN POWER?

One of the most promising new technologies that draws on coal is hydrogen fuel. Hydrogen-powered cars use fuel cells, not electric batteries, to provide power to the engine. The fuel cells can be replenished in a very short time, much shorter than the time needed to recharge a battery-powered vehicle. It takes just a few minutes, for example, to refill the hydrogen cells in a Toyota Mirai. Another plus is that hydrogen combustion emits no carbon dioxide or other toxic pollutants into the atmosphere, although the current production process does send carbon dioxide and other greenhouse gases into the atmosphere.

To encourage car buyers, some states offer tax credits or rebates to individuals buying hydrogen- or electric-powered cars. The Clean Vehicle Rebate Project in California, for example, offers a rebate of up to $6,500 for those who buy a zero-emission vehicle, including hydrogen fuel cell cars such as the Honda Clarity or the Hyundai Tucson.[10]

A drawback as of 2016 was that hydrogen stations, either standing alone or placed at existing gas stations, were still hard to find for ordinary drivers. But many manufacturers see hydrogen

*Hydrogen stations must become widespread for the technology to take off.*

as a promising vehicle technology, and hydrogen-powered buses, trains, motorcycles, wheelchairs, and even golf carts have started rolling off assembly lines.

The key ingredient in this picture is coal, which can be transformed into hydrogen through the process of gasification. If hydrogen power emerges as a key vehicle technology, the coal industry will be able to expand its market in the United States and around the world. Many struggling coal companies will be able to retain their workers and stay in business.

Not all energy observers agree that hydrogen fuel cells are environmentally friendlier than electric vehicles. The production of hydrogen involves the mining of fossil fuels and the release of carbon dioxide into the atmosphere. According to one report, "Hydrogen cannot be extracted from the ground without simultaneously extracting and disposing of carbon as CO2 [carbon dioxide]. Re-capturing the carbon (sequestering CO2) costs about the same as the resulting hydrogen fuel and hence it is simply released into the atmosphere."[11]

For thousands of years, humans have been using coal to generate heat and, more recently, light and electric power. In energy history, the Fossil Fuel Age is now giving way to the Renewable Age. But coal will survive as a useful resource. Scientists and businesses will develop solutions for coal's environmental impacts. In addition, this abundant black rock will continue to play a role in energy production, as well as new energy technologies.

# COAL PRODUCTION 2014[12]

**② UNITED STATES**
**1,000 million short tons**
(907 million metric tons)

N
W ◈ E
S

**GERMANY**
**205 million short tons**
(186 million metric tons)

**RUSSIA**
**395 million short tons**
(358 million metric tons)

**POLAND**
**151 million short tons**
(137 million metric tons)

**CHINA**
**4,270 million short tons**
(3,874 million metric tons)

**INDONESIA**
**505 million short tons**
(458 million metric tons)

**KAZAKHSTAN**
**120 million short tons**
(109 million metric tons)

**INDIA**
**710 million short tons**
(644 million metric tons)

**AUSTRALIA**
**542 million short tons**
(492 million metric tons)

**SOUTH AFRICA**
**288 million short tons**
(261 million metric tons)

# Timeline

## 1300s
Newcastle in northeastern England develops the first commercial coal mining industry.

## 1748
North America's first commercial coal mining begins in Virginia.

## 1830s
Coal replaces wood as the most important fuel source for locomotive engines.

## 1866
The first strip coal mines begin production near Danville, Illinois.

## 1882
Thomas Edison starts the operation of the first commercial electric generating station, powered by coal furnaces, on Pearl Street in New York City.

## 1890
Labor leaders establish the United Mine Workers, a union of coal miners, in Columbus, Ohio.

## 1907
An explosion at the Monongah mine in West Virginia kills 361 men and boys—the worst mine accident in US history.

## 1921
An insurrection at Blair Mountain in southern West Virginia pits coal miners against coal company enforcers as well as the US military.

## 1966

Surface mining begins at the Black Mesa mine in northeastern Arizona.

## 1969

The Federal Coal Mine Health and Safety Act is passed. The law sets down safety regulations for surface mines and allows miners with black lung disease to receive disability benefits.

## 1977

The federal Surface Mining Control and Reclamation Act requires the reclamation of land used for aboveground coal mines.

## 2009

American Electric Power builds the first US carbon capture and storage operation at its Mountaineer plant in West Virginia.

## 2016

Arch Coal and Peabody Energy, the two largest US coal producers, file for bankruptcy protection.

# Essential Facts

## IMPACT ON HISTORY

Coal has been used for home heating since the time of the Roman Empire. It was used as the principle fuel for steam engines and locomotives during the Industrial Revolution. Coal played a key role in the rise of the modern electric power industry, and it still fuels more than one-third of all power plants in the United States.

## KEY FIGURES

- Arch Coal is one of the largest coal companies in the United States; it filed for bankruptcy in 2016.

- Samuel Insull created utility companies that helped make electricity common in US homes, driving the demand for coal.

- The United Mine Workers union and its leaders including John Mitchell and John L. Lewis pushed for better protections for miners.

## KEY STATISTICS

*US Coal Industry Statistics, 2014*

▸ Total Coal Mined: 1,000,049,000 short tons (907,229,192 metric tons)

▸ Total Production Capacity: 1,243,700,000 short tons (1,128,265,661 metric tons)

▸ Number of Mines: 985

▸ Most Productive Mine: North Antelope Rochelle Mine, Wyoming

▸ Major Producers: Peabody Energy, Arch Coal, Cloud Peak Energy, Alpha Natural Resources, Murray Energy Corporation

▸ Employees: 74,931

## QUOTE

"It is widely agreed coal is set to stay in the energy mix for a long time to come because there is no alternative solution that can provide reasonably priced electricity."

*–Coaltrans World Coal Leaders Network industry conference, 2015*

# Glossary

**acid rain**

Damaging precipitation with a high concentration of sulfur dioxide and other compounds.

**dragline**

A large excavator using huge buckets and long wire cables for surface mining.

**dynamo**

A machine that generates electric current.

**embargo**

A government order that restricts the trade of one or more commodities or goods.

**feedstock**

A fuel source, such as coal or natural gas, used in power plants.

**forge**

A furnace used to heat metal, allowing it to be shaped.

**kilowatt-hour**

The production of 1,000 watts of electricity for one hour, the key measure of output by power plants.

## R/P ratio

Reserves-to-production ratio, showing the remaining amount of recoverable coal from a single source.

## reclamation

A process of restoring the natural environment after surface mining.

## subsidiary

A company that is owned and largely controlled by another company.

## syngas

Synthetic gas made from low-grade coal.

# Additional Resources

## SELECTED BIBLIOGRAPHY

Bryce, Robert. *Power Hungry: The Myths of "Green" Energy and the Real Fuels of the Future*. New York: Public Affairs, 2011. Print.

Goodell, Jeff. *Big Coal: The Dirty Secret Behind America's Energy Future*. Boston: Mariner, 2007. Print.

Shnayerson, Michael. *Coal River*. New York: Farrar, 2008. Print.

## FURTHER READINGS

Lusted, Marcia Amidon. *The Chilean Miners' Rescue*. Minneapolis: Abdo, 2012. Print.

Nelson, S. D. *Digging a Hole to Heaven: Coal Miner Boys*. New York: Abrams, 2014. Print.

Ruby, Lois. *Strike! Mother Jones and the Colorado Coal Field War*. Palmer Lake, CO: Filter, 2012. Print.

## WEBSITES

To learn more about Big Business, visit **booklinks.abdopublishing.com**. These links are routinely monitored and updated to provide the most current information available.

# FOR MORE INFORMATION

For more information on this subject, contact or visit the following organizations:

## Kentucky Coal Museum and Portal 31

231 Main Street
Benham, KY 40807
606-848-1530
http://www.benhamky.org/Museum/

This museum features exhibits on the local coal industry and the company towns of Benham and Lynch. Portal 31, in nearby Lynch, is Kentucky's first exhibition coal mine.

## Museum of Science and Industry

5700 S Lake Shore Drive
Chicago, IL 60637
773-684-1414
http://www.msichicago.org/explore/whats-here/exhibits/coal-mine/

One of the most popular exhibits at the Museum of Science and Industry in Chicago is its oldest exhibit, the Coal Mine. Visitors ride an elevator down into this real mine, which was relocated to the museum from southern Illinois.

# Source Notes

## CHAPTER 1. COAL AND SOCIETY

1. Ronald D. Eller. *Miners, Millhands, and Mountaineers: Industrialization of the Appalachian South, 1880–1930*. Knoxville, TN: U of Tennessee P, 1982. 156. *Google Book Search*. Web. 1 Aug. 2016.

2. "Coal Explained: Coal Prices and Outlook." *US Energy Information Administration*. US Department of Energy, 14 Dec. 2015. Web. 1 Aug. 2016.

3. "Coal Prices and Charts." *Quandl*. Quandl, 15 June 2016. Web. 20 June 2016.

4. Andrew Topf. "5 Reasons Why Coal Is Being Killed Off." *Oilprice.com*. Oilprice.com, 11 Dec. 2015. Web. 1 Aug. 2016.

5. Keith Epstein. "Decades after Clean Air Act, Most Smokestacks Still Lack Scrubbers." *The Center for Public Integrity*. The Center for Public Integrity, 19 May 2014. Web. 1 Aug. 2016.

6. American Coal Foundation. "Types of Coal." *Electronic Trip to a Coal Mine*. Kentucky Educational Television, 15 Dec. 2005. Web. 1 Aug. 2016.

7. "Frequently Asked Questions: How Much Coal, Natural Gas, or Petroleum Is Used to Generate a Kilowatthour of Electricity?" *US Energy Information Administration*. US Department of Energy, 29 Feb. 2016. Web. 1 Aug. 2016.

8. "How Is Steel Produced?" *World Coal Association*. World Coal Association, 2016. Web. 1 Aug. 2016.

9. "What Next for Coal?" *World Coal*. Palladian Publications, 28 Oct. 2015. Web. 1 Aug. 2016.

## CHAPTER 2. WHAT IS COAL?

1. "Quarterly Coal Report (Abbreviated) January–March 2016." *US Energy Information Administration*. US Department of Energy, June 2016. Web. 1 Aug. 2016. 2.

2. "Coal in Indiana." *Indiana Geological Survey*. The Trustees of Indiana University, 2015. Web. 1 Aug. 2016.

3. "Coal Reserves." *BP Global*. BP, 2016. Web. 1 Aug. 2016.

4. "World Coal Production by Year." *Index Mundi*. Index Mundi, 2016. Web. 1 Aug. 2016.

5. "Coal Mining." *World Coal Association*. World Coal Association, 2016. Web. 1 Aug. 2016.

6. "BP Statistical Review of World Energy June 2015." *BP*. BP, June 2015. Web. 1 Aug. 2016. 30.

7. Charles Kennedy. "Goldman Sachs: 'Peak Coal' Is Here." *Oilprice.com*. Oilprice.com, 24 Sept. 2015. Web. 1 Aug. 2016.

8. Thomas Spencer. "The Future of Coal: The Long Comedown." *Energy Post*. Energy Post, 17 Nov. 2015. Web. 1 Aug. 2016.

## CHAPTER 3. THE COAL REVOLUTION

1. "Coal in Virginia." *VirginiaPlaces.org*. Professor Charlie Grymes, n.d. Web. 1 Aug. 2016.

2. Matthew White. "The Industrial Revolution." *British Library*. British Library Board, n.d. Web. 1 Aug. 2016.

3. "This Day in History, 1876: Hundreds Die in Brooklyn Theater Fire." *History*. A&E Television, 2016. Web. 1 Aug. 2016.

5. Roger Lowenstein. "Before There Was Enron, There Was Insull." *New York Times*. New York Times, 19 Mar. 2006. Web. 1 Aug. 2016.

6. "Peabody at a Glance." *Peabody Energy*. Peabody Energy, 2014. Web. 1 Aug. 2016.

## CHAPTER 4. THE COAL INDUSTRY GROWS

1. "History of Mine Safety and Health Legislation." *Mine Safety and Health Administration*. US Department of Labor, n.d. Web. 1 Aug. 2016.

2. "This Day in History, 1907: The Monongah Mine Disaster." *History*. A&E Television, 2016. Web. 1 Aug. 2016.

3. "Blair Mountain: The History of a Confrontation." *Preservation Alliance of West Virginia*. Preservation Alliance of West Virginia, 2006. Web. 1 Aug. 2016.

4. "Coal Reignites a Mighty Battle of Labor History." *All Things Considered*. National Public Radio, 5 Mar. 2011. Web. 1 Aug. 2016.

5. "1974, Early Coal Miner's Wages and Striking." *Marion Illinois History Preservation*. Marion Illinois History Preservation, 15 Dec. 2013. Web. 1 Aug. 2016.

6. "Annual Coal Mining Wages vs. All Industries, 2013." *National Mining Association*. National Mining Association, 2013. Web. 1 Aug. 2016.

7. "Today in Energy: Natural Gas Expected to Surpass Coal in Mix of Fuel Used for US Power Generation in 2016." *US Energy Information Administration*. US Department of Energy, 16 Mar. 2016. Web. 1 Aug 2016.

8. Stephen Castle. "Lights Out in Britain for the Coal Industry." *New York Times*. New York Times, 31 Oct. 2015. Web. 1 Aug. 2016.

9. "Backgrounder on Chernobyl Nuclear Power Plant Accident." *US Nuclear Regulatory Commission*. US Nuclear Regulatory Commission, 12 Dec. 2014. Web. 1 Aug. 2016.

10. "Power Sector at a Glance, All India." *Ministry of Power*. Government of India, 20 July 2016. Web. 1 Aug. 2016.

11. "Today in Energy: China Produces and Consumes Almost as Much Coal as the Rest of the World Combined." *US Energy Information Administration*. US Department of Energy, 14 May 2014. Web. 1 Aug. 2016.

12. K. Jayalakshmi. "China: Thousands Protest against Coal-Fired Power Plant in Heyuan." *International Business Times*. IBTimes, 13 Apr. 2015. Web. 1 Aug. 2016.

## CHAPTER 5. DIGGING COAL

1. "Reclamation: Did You Know?" *NMA*. National Mining Association, 2015. Web. 1 Aug. 2016.

2. Judith Nies. "The Black Mesa Syndrome: Indian Lands, Black Gold." *Orion Magazine*. Orion Magazine, Summer 1998. Web. 1 Aug. 2016.

## CHAPTER 6. COAL HAZARDS

1. J. Davitt McAteer and Associates. "Report to the Governor: Upper Big Branch." *Governor's Independent Investigation Panel*. Governor of West Virginia, May 2011. Web. 1 Aug. 2016. 17.

2. "Quecreek Mine Rescue Facts." *CNN*. CNN, 3 Mar. 2016. Web. 1 Aug. 2016.

# Source Notes Continued

3. J. Davitt McAteer and Associates. "Report to the Governor: Upper Big Branch." *Governor's Independent Investigation Panel*. Governor of West Virginia, May 2011. Web. 1 Aug. 2016. 4.

4. Ibid. 21.

5. Ian Urbina. "No Survivors Found After West Virginia Mine Disaster." *New York Times*. New York Times, 10 Apr. 2010. Web. 1 Aug. 2016.

6. Michael J. Brnich Jr. and Kathleen M. Kowalski-Trakofker. "Underground Coal Mine Disasters 1900–2010: Events, Responses, and a Look to the Future." *NIOSH Office of Mine Safety and Health*. CDC, Jan. 2010. Web. 1 Aug. 2016. 3.

7. "US Labor Department's MSHA Cites Corporate Culture as Root Cause of Upper Big Branch Mine Disaster." *Mine Safety and Health Administration*. United States Department of Labor, 6 Dec. 2011. Web. 1 Aug. 2016.

8. J. Davitt McAteer and Associates. "Report to the Governor: Upper Big Branch." *Governor's Independent Investigation Panel*. Governor of West Virginia, May 2011. Web. 1 Aug. 2016. 4.

9. "US Labor Department's MSHA Cites Corporate Culture as Root Cause of Upper Big Branch Mine Disaster." *Mine Safety and Health Administration*. US Department of Labor, 6 Dec. 2011. Web. 1 Aug. 2016.

10. Jeff Goodell. *Big Coal: The Dirty Secret behind America's Energy Future*. Boston: Mariner, 2007. Print. 53.

11. D. Pappas and C. Mark. "A Deeper Look at Contractor Injuries in Underground Coal Mines." *NIOSH Office of Mine Safety and Health*. CDC, 2011. Web. 1 Aug. 2016.

12. Mark J. Perry. "Chart of the Day: Coal Mining Deaths in the US, 1900–2013." *AEI Ideas*. American Enterprise Institute, 15 May 2014. Web. 1 Aug. 2016.

## CHAPTER 7. GLOBAL WARMING AND CLEAN COAL

1. "Coal." *Center for Climate and Energy Solutions*. Center for Climate and Energy Solutions, n.d. Web. 1 Aug. 2016.

2. "Time Series: Climate at a Glance." *National Centers for Environmental Information*. NOAA, n.d. Web. 1 Aug. 2016.

3. Jon Erdman. "February 2016 Was the Most Abnormally Warm Month on Record, NOAA and NASA Say." *The Weather Channel*. The Weather Channel, 17 Mar. 2016. Web. 1 Aug. 2016.

4. "An Introduction to the Science of Climate Change." *Transportation and Climate Change Clearinghouse*. US Department of Transportation, n.d. Web. 1 Aug. 2016.

5. "Is Current Warming Natural?" *Earth Observatory*. NASA, n.d. Web. 1 Aug. 2016.

6. "Coal." *Center for Climate and Energy Solutions*. Center for Climate and Energy Solutions, n.d. Web. 1 Aug. 2016.

7. Brian Ricketts. "Coal Industry Stands for Progress and Prosperity." *EurActiv*. EurActiv, 27 Feb. 2015. Web. 1 Aug. 2016.

8. "Coal." *Center for Climate and Energy Solutions*. Center for Climate and Energy Solutions, n.d. Web. 1 Aug. 2016.

9. Richard Anderson. "Coal Gasification: The Clean Energy of the Future?" *BBC*. BBC, 14 Apr. 2014. Web. 1 Aug. 2016.

## CHAPTER 8. NEW COAL TECHNOLOGIES

1. "Sulfur Dioxide Trends." *US Environmental Protection Agency*. US EPA, 21 July 2016. Web. 1 Aug. 2016.

2. Michelle Nijhuis. "Can Coal Ever Be Clean?" *National Geographic*. National Geographic, Apr. 2014. Web. 1 Aug. 2016.

3. The White House. "Fact Sheet: US Reports Its 2025 Emissions Target to the UNFCCC." *Briefing Room*. The White House, 31 Mar. 2015. Web. 1 Aug. 2016.

4. Michelle Nijhuis. "Can Coal Ever Be Clean?" *National Geographic*. National Geographic, Apr. 2014. Web. 1 Aug. 2016.

5. "AEP Places Carbon Capture Commercialization on Hold, Citing Uncertain Status of Climate Policy, Weak Economy." *American Electric Power*. AEP, 14 July 2011. Web. 1 Aug. 2016.

6. "What Is CCS: Storage." *Global CCS Institute*. Global CCS Institute, n.d. Web. 1 Aug. 2016.

7. Nicholas Ducote and H. Sterling Burnett. "Turning Coal into Liquid Fuel." *National Center for Policy Analysis*. National Center for Policy Analysis, 1 May 2009. Web. 1 Aug. 2016.

8. Dr. Fred C. Beach. "Coal Liquefaction." *Lecture Notes, Energy and Technology Policy (ChE 359/384)*. University of Texas at Austin, 1 Oct. 2013. Web. 1 Aug. 2016.

9. Myra P. Saefong. "Oil Ends under $40 as Doha Talks Collapse." *Market Watch*. Market Watch, 18 Apr. 2016. Web. 1 Aug. 2016.

10. "China Shenhua Energy Company Limited." *International Directory of Company Histories*. Thomson Gale, 2007. Web. 1 Aug. 2016.

11. J. William Carpenter. "The 7 Biggest Chinese Mining Companies." *Investopedia*. Investopedia. 16 Sept. 2015. Web. 1 Aug. 2016.

## CHAPTER 9. THE FUTURE OF COAL

1. Lindsay Wilson. "Average Household Electricity Use around the World." *Shrink That Footprint*. Shrink That Footprint, n.d. Web. 1 Aug. 2016.

2. "Electric Power Annual: Table 4.1, Count of Electric Power Industry Power Plants, by Sector, by Predominant Energy Sources within Plant." *US Energy Information Administration*. US Department of Energy, 16 Feb. 2016. Web. 1 Aug. 2016.

3. "Coal Prices and Charts." *Quandl*. Quandl, 15 June 2016. Web. 20 June 2016.

4. "Fast Facts about Coal." *Rocky Mountain Coal Mining Institute*. RMCMI, n.d. Web. 1 Aug. 2016.

5. John W. Miller and Peg Brickley. "Arch Coal Files for Bankruptcy." *Wall Street Journal*. Dow Jones, 11 Jan. 2016. Web. 1 Aug. 2016.

6. Ibid.

7. Nick Dewey. "Selling Energy Back to the Grid Using Home Made Solar Panels." *YouTube*. YouTube, 9 Aug. 2011. Web. 1 Aug. 2016.

8. Tom Zeller Jr. and Stefan Milkowski. "Burning Coal at Home Is Making a Comeback." *New York Times*. New York Times, 26 Dec. 2008. Web. 1 Aug. 2016.

9. Jordan Weissmann. "The Solar Business Now Employs More Americans Than Coal." *Slate*. Slate, 23 Feb. 2015. Web. 1 Aug. 2016.

10. "California Clean Vehicle Rebate Project." *California Air Resources Board*. Center for Sustainable Energy, 2016. Web. 1 Aug. 2016.

11. Julian Cox. "Time to Come Clean about Hydrogen Fuel Cell Vehicles." *Clean Technica*. Clean Technica, 4 June 2014. Web. 1 Aug. 2016.

12. "BP Statistical Review of World Energy." *British Petroleum*. BP, June 2016. Web. 14 Sept. 2016.

# Index

## ABOUT THE AUTHOR

Tom Streissguth has written more than 100 nonfiction books for young people. He has worked as a journalist, teacher, and editor, and he is the founder of the Archive of American Journalism, which publishes long-neglected works of authors such as Mark Twain, Jack London, and Ernest Hemingway. He lives in Woodbury, Minnesota.